Anointing Oils for the Bride

by

Elsabe Briers

ANOINTING OILS FOR THE BRIDE
ALLEGORY OF THE BOOK OF ESTHER
by
Elsabe Briers

JACKSONVILLE
FLORIDA

E-mail: agapelifeworld@juno.com

All Scripture quotations are taken from the
New King James Version of the Bible.

Printed in the United States of America

©2003 Elsabe Briers

ISBN #1-889668-26-5

All rights reserved. No portion of this book may be reproduced in any form without written consent of the author. For ordering information, please contact the publisher:

    Smith & Daniel Marketing / Book Division
    4981 Atlantic Blvd. #9
    Jacksonville, Florida 32207
    telephone 1-800-330-1325

Acknowledgements

I give all glory and thanks to the Triune God who, by the Holy Spirit, drew me with cords of love into the intimacy of the bridal chambers.

My heartfelt appreciation and thanks also to everyone who helped with the editing and publishing of the book and my thanks to my brothers and sisters in the Lord whose prayers, encouragement and support have made this book possible to be used for the glory of God.

Foreword

By Drs. Bob & Glenyce Doorn
Ministers of the Gospel for over 50 years
to the nations of the world.

We met the author, Elsabe, and her youngest daughter, Cavelle, who are from South Africa, not by chance but by the destiny of God. Cavelle became, as it were, a spiritual granddaughter to us and is now in fulltime Christian Service at the World Headquarters of the Endtime Handmaidens and Servants in Arkansas, U.S.A.

Upon reading this lovely book, we at once discovered the true heart of this Handmaiden of the Lord, Elsabe. She expresses the love and longing for Jesus as her Heavenly Bridegroom in such a way that it also imparts that same love and longing in one's own heart.

Analogies taken from the life of Queen Esther and the word pictures so vividly painted in this book express what ought to be the desire of every spiritual believer – to be more like Jesus.

The following pages will inspire the reader to seek after such a life that will forever be pleasing to God and bring about an Eternal Reward.

Introduction

In the book of Esther we find the portrayal of the soul's journey from darkness into light, from the world into the chambers of the Beloved, learning the principles of the Kingdom of His Love.

This journey is an answer to His call that takes us from the initial surrender, on a path of many altars, through the wilderness to the Promised Land of His glorious presence. Here we live a life of worship in union with the King as His Bride.

Though there are giants in this land, He gives us the victory through the death of self and empowers us for the commission to bring Life and Light to the nations.

At the same time, we are being prepared, as the overcoming Church, to be the glorious spotless Bride for the marriage feast of the Lamb.

This is a message of God to the end-time Church!

It is by no means an attempt to paint the whole picture of the Book of Esther, but it brings a challenge to the believers to yield their lives fully to the leading of the Holy Spirit in order to fulfill God's purpose and calling in their lives.

I sincerely believe with all my heart that this is a call to those who desire the bridal anointing, to rise to their destiny.

Compelled by Love, the Bride wills to be separated from the world for a preparation and cleansing to the point of death to self. This is needful in order to be a vessel filled with His anointing and with the authority of the King's seal for the *greater works* that He has prepared, to bring in the end-time harvest and confound the plans of the enemy against God's people.

There is a wakeup call for the Bride of Christ!

The Father's heart is yearning for the Bride to be made ready for the Bridegroom, for the marriage feast of the Lamb.

There is electricity in the air. This expectation causes a bubbling in our spirits! This is the time of preparation for the Bride through the fires of testing and trials. It brings forth treasures of gold on the inside for those who are willing to be purged from dross. We are being clothed with holiness, in bridal attire and the anointing oils are being poured out freely on those who live to worship the Bridegroom in Spirit and in Truth. The time for union with the King of kings has come. We, His people are lovesick for the Beloved, and our adoration ravishes His heart (Songs 4:9).

Halleluiah! The Bride is rising up in glory! Out of this love union with the Father and the Son through the Holy Spirit, our hearts are put on fire with His passion for souls. We acquire a vision for the nations and in our mind's eye we can see the sickle in the harvest fields of the world, taking our part in it, fulfilling our destiny for such a time as this. In the river of His glory we cry out in intercession for souls and we prophesy salvation and revival to the nations at the mercy seat of God.

> **Put on your strength, put on your beautiful garments, oh Bride!**
> **Shake yourself from the dust, arise!**
> **Break forth into joy, sing together,**
> **For the Lord has comforted His People**
> **You have been redeemed by the Blood of the Lamb!**
> — *Isaiah 52: 1,2,9*

Let us now live in resurrection power of the Holy Spirit and abide in His Presence, His Word and His Love!

We have been seated together with Christ Jesus in heavenly places (Ephesians 2) to rule over our enemies in His Name and by the power of the Lamb's Blood.

We have a testimony because we are *overcomers* through the Blood of the Lamb and do not love our lives, even unto death (Revelation 12: 11). Halleluiah!

Contents

1. A Little About "Allegories, Types and Shadows" 1
2. The Calling of Esther 5
3. Surrender, Obedience and Altars 7
4. Vision 14
5. The Anointing Oils and the Bridal Attire 21
   Suffering 22
   Brokenness 24
   Myrrh as an Embalming Spice for the Dead 25
   The Garment of Salvation & the Robe of Righteousness 26
   Fire Precedes the Glory 28
   The Garment of Praise & The Oil of Joy for Mourning. 29
   Faith in the Fire 32
   Attitude in the Waiting Room 35
   More Altars 36
   The Love Anointing 37
6. Time and Timing in the Waiting Room 45
7. More Ingredients of the Anointing Oils 48
8. Scent for Our Garments 54
9. The Altar of Incense 58

10. The Bridal Tent 63
11. Plans and Strategies of the Enemy of Our Souls 78
12. Prophetic Worship 82
13. Feasting with the King in the
    Presence of My Enemies 88
14. Victory Over the Enemy 94
15. The Bride without Spot or Wrinkle 102

1

A Little About "Allegories, Types and Shadows"

The book of Esther can be read as an event in history or interpreted as an allegory with type and shadow of things to come.

As an *allegory,* this is "a story in which the people, things and events have a symbolic meaning: *allegories* are used for teaching or explaining ideas, morals or principles." (Webster's Dictionary)

A *type (or shadow, a figure, model)* – "a person, thing, or event that represents another, especially another that it is thought will appear later; symbol; token; sign." (Webster's Dictionary)

Esther is the beautiful orphaned Jewess who became the queen of the Persian king, Ahasueros. She is a type of the Bride of Christ in the Church, separated from the world and totally surrendered to the Holy Spirit, going through a process of purging and cleansing in the river of His glory where she is anointed to be brought in union with her Bridegroom, King Jesus. At the same time she is being equipped with the weapons of warfare to take dominion over the works of darkness in the name and authority of the King, while she is positionally seated in heavenly places in Christ Jesus at the right hand of the Father.

She is also a type of the body of believers within the Church who is separated (in the river of purification) from the religious church system. So to speak, while she is being soaked in the anointing oils, at the prescription of the Holy Spirit, she is being transformed into the image of Christ. She is a servant to His body, while the Lord ministers through her, by the gifts of the Holy Spirit to the poor, the brokenhearted and the captives, that they can be set free to enjoy their inheritance with the saints. She is prepared both to fulfill her predestined call here on earth as *more than victorious* against the wiles and strategies of the enemy, and as part of the glorious, overcoming Church, ready to rule and reign with Christ.

Mordecai, the uncle of Esther, is a type of the Holy Spirit, guiding, counseling, watching and hovering over Esther as his charge. His aim is to have her refined and polished in all aspects of her character to be made ready as Bride for the heavenly Bridegroom – to be changed into the image of the King - and for her to fulfill her destiny for which she was predestined, called, justified and glorified.

Hegai, the custodian of the women, personifies the work of the Holy Spirit in the "inward parts," giving the prescriptions for the renewing of the mind, ministering to Esther's character as she,

> *"with unveiled face, beholding as in a mirror the glory of the Lord, is being transformed into the same image from glory to glory, just as by the Spirit of the Lord."*
> *2 Corinthians 3: 18*

Vashti means *"fair"* and it is clear that she was *taken out* of her position by the Providence of God, because the time had come for someone like Esther to be put into position for the deliverance of God's people out of the hand of their enemy. Vashti could also be seen as representing the old order or tradition of the law, which had to be replaced by the new order of grace, represented by Esther.

The seven choice maidservants: The number seven stands for perfection and the maidservants portray the chosen, Holy Spirit appointed ministries that speak into our lives, minister to us, pray for us, reprimand us in love, exhort us and encourage us so that we can be made ready for the Bridegroom – a Bride *not having spot or wrinkle.*

Ahasueros, the king, is a type of our heavenly Bridegroom, Jesus and is portrayed in Chapter 1 of the book of Esther in all his kingly splendor and riches.

Haman, the prince and the king's second in command, can be seen as two-fold type – firstly he represents the fallen, prideful and selfish human nature and secondly, being given over to the lusts of the flesh, he becomes the tool in the hands of satan, motivated by him to steal, kill and destroy God's people.

Shushan literally means "palace" (the dwelling place of the king) and "city of lilies." The word "lily" is symbolical of the Bride of Christ, representing a sweet fragrance, purity and beauty.

Shushan - poetically, the kingdom where the "lilies" are grown.

The heart of the Bride and of the Church is represented by Shushan, as the habitation of the King and the desire of the Holy Spirit is expressed in the events, to be given full reign over the dwelling place of the King.

The desire of the Father's heart, is to have a glorious Bride for His Son, washed in the blood of the Lamb, without spot or wrinkle, prepared by the Holy Spirit for the marriage feast of the Lamb where after she will rule and reign with Him forever.

The Bridegroom wants a Bride in His image, in union with Him and the Father, sanctified, full of His joy and His love – an overcoming Bride, all glorious with His glory.

The Holy Spirit is looking for those with a humble servant heart, calling us into the inner chamber of fellowship with the Father and the Son. Here He teaches us and ministers to us to be a Bride made ready for the Bridegroom.

The first part of our preparation is that of discipline through our trials and tribulations until our only desire is to please the King by choosing His will in the finest details of our lives; the second half is to anoint us as worshippers of the Bridegroom, carrying the fragrance of the incense, being filled with His glory to be brought in union with Him.

2

The Calling of Esther

*"For you see your calling, brethren, that not many wise according to the flesh, not many mighty, not many noble, are called. But God has chosen the foolish things of the world to put to shame the wise, and God has chosen the weak things of the world to put to shame the things which are mighty; and the base things of the world and the things which are despised God has chosen, and the things which are not, to bring to nothing the things that are, **that no flesh should glory in His presence.**"*
                                                       1 Corinthians 1: 26-29

Esther was an unknown orphan, but God had brought her from obscurity and had destined her to become the queen - the instrument in His mighty hand for setting her people free. She had no "name" or fame, no reputation or earthly qualification, but she was chosen and predestined by God to fulfill His purpose because she had a humble heart, ready to do His will.

"Christ in you, the hope of glory."
                                                       Collosians 1: 27

In this same way Rebekah was chosen as Bride for Isaac. She found favor because of her *willingness to serve in humility.*

God's eyes are upon those whose hearts are loyal to Him, who show their love to Him in obedience and submission to His will.

"For the eyes of the Lord run to and fro throughout the whole earth, to show Himself strong on behalf of those whose heart is loyal to Him."
2 Chronicles 16: 9

With the call there is a destiny involved!

*"For whom He foreknew, He also **predestined** to be conformed to the image of His Son, that He might be the firstborn among many brethren. Moreover whom He predestined, these He also **called**; whom He called, He also **justified**; and whom He justified, He also **glorified**."*
Romans 8: 29-30

Let us therefore not look at our ability or earthly heritage, our qualifications or reputation in order to think ourselves qualified for God's purposes. Let us glory in the risen Christ within us.

Are you ready to answer His call in full surrender to His will for your life?

3

Surrender, Obedience & Altars

The journey to the Bridal chamber goes through the Tabernacle of God, which is in type and shadow resembling the three-fold nature of man. The Outer Court corresponds to the body, the Holy Place resembles the soul area and the Holy of Holies represents man's spirit.

In the Outer Court, we find the brazen altar where lambs were sanctified for the atonement of sin. Symbolically, this is the place where we lay down our lives to the Lord, both in our initial choice to make Him Lord of our lives, as well as in our daily offering of ourselves to Him.

We all come to the place in our lives where we have to make the choice whether or not we will entrust our lives fully into the hands of the Lord in unconditional surrender. This seems frightening at first - as if we would lose all. And in a sense it is true – yes, we will "lose our lives", but we have to get the revelation that we will gain His life in Glory!

"Whoever desires to come after Me, let him deny himself,

> *and take up his cross, and follow Me.*
> *For whoever desires to save his life, will **lose it**, but whoever loses his life for My sake and the gospel's will **save it**.*
> *For what will it profit a man if he gains the whole world, and loses his own soul?*
> *Or what will a man give in exchange for his soul?"*
> Mark 8: 34-37

The first quality we find in this young girl, Esther, is *humble submission to godly authority*. She had been raised in the fear of God, under the care of her uncle, Mordecai, who is a type of the Holy Spirit. When he decided to take her to the king's palace, she was prepared to give up her own agenda, her identity, her dreams and plans and everything that was part of her background, in *obedience* and *submission* to Mordecai. In the Jewish culture it was their custom that a marriage be arranged by the parents and therefore it could be expected that Esther would submit to Mordecai's discretion, since he was her custodian.

Her name was changed from Hadassah ("Myrtle") to Esther ("Star"), as she was charged not to reveal her people or family.

The changing of a name in the Bible often occurred when someone stepped out in faith to obey the call of God. Abram became Abraham, Sarai became Sarah; Jacob's name was changed to Israel; Simon's name was changed to Peter.

A change of name also implies a prophetic proclamation of the person's destiny. When Hadassah's name was changed to Esther, her *divine destiny* was proclaimed every time someone called her name. The beauty of her natural life (Hadassah means "Myrtle" – a green shrub) had to be exchanged for the Holy Spirit's life in her that would radiate the beauty of His Glory, like a star reflecting the light of the sun. We have been called out of darkness into the light and now we are to shine His light into the darkness of the world.

> *"Those who are wise shall shine*
> *Like the brightness of the firmament,*
> *And those who turn many to righteousness*
> *Like the stars forever and ever."*
>
> Daniel 12: 3

If we want to fulfill our destiny and walk in the Glory of the Lord, we have to be prepared to die to everything of self and selfish desires – if required, also to leave our homes, family, security and even our country to answer the call of Christ through the guidance of the Holy Spirit.

> *".... whoever of you does not forsake all that he has cannot be My disciple."*
>
> Luke 14: 33

Emotional ties to people - where we have clung to our loved ones for emotional security - have to be severed. We should not hold on to a human being, neither should we allow anyone to cling to us for emotional security. Instead, we have to put all our trust in the Lord and be entwined with Him, becoming one with Him.

Intertwined with *consecration* is *sacrifice*. When we look at the lives of the great men and women of God, we see that their journeys are marked with altars.

An altar is a place of *sacrifice*, a place of *covenant*, and a place of *worship*.

Everywhere God meets with man, an altar is required - obedience brings death to self!

When, at first, we surrender our lives to the Lord, we think that all is on the altar, but very quickly we discover that there are Baal altars of idolatry in our lives that need to be torn down and in their place God wants us to build an altar for Him; likewise, the wooden images of our dead works need to be cut down, and the wood used for burnt offerings unto the Lord (Judges 6: 25 – 26).

> "For no other foundation can anyone lay than that which is laid, which is Jesus Christ. Now if anyone builds on this foundation with gold, silver, precious stones, wood, hay straw, each one's work will become clear; for the Day will declare it, because it will be revealed by fire; and the fire will test each one's work, of what sort it is."
>
> 1 Corinthians 3: 11-13

And naturally it follows that the sacrifice is asking for the fire of God to consume it so that it can be justified and then glorified. This is the way all of our preconceived ideas, "issues", problems, sins and hang-ups have to go - to the altar, to be consumed by the fire of God for His glory!

We have to put our very lives on the *altar of sacrifice* to be burned out by God's fire and follow the call of God for the praise of His glory.

> "In Him also we have obtained an inheritance, being predestined according to the purpose of Him who works all things according to the counsel of His will, that we who first trusted in Christ should be to the praise of His Glory."
>
> – Ephesians 1: 11-12

In Genesis 12 we see that God required the same obedience from Abram. He also had to leave his comfort zone, his country, his family and his father's house to go into an unknown land and a future known only by his God. This was the sacrifice of his own life; later on he would be required to sacrifice all the promises of God that had been given to him in his son, Isaac. His security was the faithfulness of God.

*"Most assuredly, I say to you,
unless a grain of wheat falls into the ground and dies,
it remains alone; but if it dies, it produces much grain.
He who loves his life will lose it,
and him who hates his life in this world
will keep it for eternal life."*

John 12: 25-26

The life of self consists of the will, thoughts and emotions, which must be brought to death and exchanged for the life of Christ.

*"For we who live are always delivered
to death for Jesus' sake, that the
life of Jesus also may be
manifested in our mortal flesh.
So death is working in us, but life in you."*

2 Corinthians 4: 11-12

Most of all, we have to make the choice to leave the past behind and not talk about it anymore, but set our eyes on the vision that God has for us, following the dictates of the Holy Spirit.

Paul speaks of
*"forgetting those things which are behind and
reaching forward to those things which are ahead,
pressing toward the goal for the prize of the upward*

call of God in Christ Jesus."
Philippians 4: 13

To leave the past behind requires great discipline in the thought life by the power of the Holy Spirit. If we want to make progress in the kingdom of God, we have to let go of the things that are behind us. We have to "forgive and forget," and release the people, places, things and regretted issues of our *yesterdays,* live *today* yielded to the guidance and dealings of the Holy Spirit, while *tomorrow* is filled with a vision of hope.

And do not forget to forgive yourself for your failures and past mistakes. Release yourself from condemnation over the past and see yourself as God sees you. Jesus has paid the price for your redemption in order that He can have you as His Bride. Do not look over your shoulder like Lot's wife, for past regrets and emotional issues can turn us into pillars of salt where we stagnate forever and lose the inheritance of the Promised Land.

"But what things were gain to me, these I have counted loss for Christ."
Philippians 3: 7

Whenever man is put before the choice between God and something else - God and money, God and human love, God and self, God and personal ambition, God and men's opinion, the true condition of his heart will be exposed.

We are reminded of that old song:

I have decided to follow Jesus

I have decided to follow Jesus
I have decided to follow Jesus
No turning back, praise the Lord
No turning back.

The cross before me,
The world behind me
The cross before me,
The world behind me

The cross before me
The world behind me
No turning back, praise the Lord
No turning back.

It will cost me everything!

Have I really surrendered all to Him?

4

Vision

Vision is the vehicle of the future. It never deals with hindsight or the present state of our circumstances. It is part of the fourth dimension of faith where we can envision the promises of God.

Vision releases purpose, commitment and focus – an embracing of something greater than yourself in a release of faith.

> *"Where there is no vision (or revelation), the people perish (or cast off restraint)."*
> Proverbs 29: 18

1. Identify with the vision

When we get a vision of God's plans for us through the Holy Spirit, the fulfillment of it many times transcends far beyond what we can pray or think. Our part is to fully commit ourselves to the Holy Spirit's discipline in order to obtain the goal.

The Holy Spirit's direction to Esther through Mordecai

was to become the bride of the king and she therefore committed herself in obedience to go through all the required preparations in order to obtain the king's favor and eventually to reign with him as his bride. She didn't realize the role that she would have to play in that which God had predestined for her in the deliverance of His people.

The fear of God, her yielding to the dictates of the Holy Spirit and her training in obedience made her able to rise to the demands of the occasion to fulfill her destiny.

Likewise we, at the outset of our spiritual journey, do not fully realize what God has in store for us, but we need to get a clear vision of the desire of the Holy Spirit to bring us in union with our heavenly Bridegroom, where we will be ready, at the appointed time, to do anything He requires of us because we love Him.

> *"And you shall love the Lord your God*
> *with all your heart, with all your soul,*
> *with all your mind, and with*
> *all your strength" and...*
> *"You shall love your neighbor as yourself"*
>
> Mark 12: 30 - 31

2. Trust in and yield fully to the guidance of the Holy Spirit

Hegai, the custodian of the women in the king's palace, portrays the guidance of the Holy Spirit, who knows what pleases the heart of the King. He gives Esther *beauty preparations* beyond her allowance because Esther *pleased Hegai* (with her *attitude* of *meekness, teachability and yieldedness*) and *she obtained his favor.* (Esther 2:9)

In our intimacy with the Holy Spirit, we learn to discern His voice, get God's vision for our lives and follow His dictates in obedience.

3. Cultivate fellowship with handmaidens and servants of the King

"Seven choice maidservants were provided for her from the king's palace."
Esther 2:9

Surround yourself with people who also love Jesus and are sold out to the King and follow the call of the Bride. They will understand the heart that is willingly surrendered to do anything and everything in order to please the King. They will minister to your needs in the King's chambers, praying and interceding for you to fulfill your destiny.

4. Separation from the world

Esther had to be willing to be separated from the world and go into the *secret place of His Presence* to be taught and anointed by the Holy Spirit. There is an open door into the Holy of Holies through the Blood of the Lamb.

Let us then enter in boldly by faith into His Presence and allow the Holy Spirit

"to create in me a clean heart and renew a steadfast spirit within me."
Psalm 51: 10

5. Write down the vision

> "Write the vision
> And make it plain on tablets,
> That he may run who reads it.
> For the vision is yet for an
> appointed time;
> But at the end it will speak, and
> It will not lie.
> Though it tarries, wait for it;
> Because it will surely come,
> It will not tarry."
>
> Habakkuk 2: 2

6. Guard the vision

We know that while we are carrying the vision of His promises and His prophetic Word on the inside of us, it grows and develops to full maturity like a baby in a womb. At first it was conceived as a seed, but as we ponder upon the Word, we water that seed and God makes it grow and brings it to birth.

In the beginning the form was vague, but in time all the functioning organs are put into place; spiritual insight is developed, spiritual hearing and understanding is cultivated and we begin to speak life to the vision until it has come to full stature. In the process, we ourselves are molded by the Potter into the desired form and then made durable in the fire to fulfill His vision and great commission.

Together, with the growth of the vision inside of us, we grow by His grace into the full stature of Christ. In His divine timing the vision is birthed.

We are often so taken up with what we think our ministry should be and we regard that as our vision, but as our intimacy with the Bridegroom grows while we worship Him in the inner sanctuary, we come to understand the higher call.

"God is faithful, by whom you were called ***into the fellowship*** *of His Son, Jesus Christ our Lord."*
1 Corinthians 1:9

In this intimacy, we are transformed by His Spirit from glory to glory into His image, with His desires, His mind, His vision and His commission so that His name can be glorified!

"Go therefore and make disciples of all the nations, baptizing them in the name of the Father and of the Son and of the Holy Spirit, teaching them to observe all things that I have commanded you; and lo, I am with you always, even to the end of the age."
Matthew 28: 19-20

> *When we seek His Kingdom first,*
> *and His Righteousness . . .*
> *all else will be added unto us!*
> *(John 6:33)*

7. Believe and envision the vision

While Esther was being prepared to reign as queen, her vision of herself in that position was growing and the more she dreamed about it, talked of it, seeing herself in that position, the more pliable and yielded she became to submit in obedience to the discipline of the Holy Spirit in order to attain His goal and purpose for her life. She had to see herself in that position by faith and practice her walk and her talk as would be required of her as the bride of the king.

> *"...so he readily gave beauty preparations to her, besides her allowance."*
>
> *Esther 2: 9*

She had to learn how to dress like a queen and her old habits that did not befit a queen had to be discarded. She had to cultivate new habits of speech. Likewise, we have to learn to have control over our tongues and speak "kingdom language" i.e. the Word of God. All our words have to bring forth life to be pleasing to the King.

All we think, do and say must be put to the test of whether it will glorify the King of kings – in other words, our hearts must be cleansed by purification.

The emphasis is shifted from "me" to Him. He becomes my whole desire, my life, my breath – the reason for making the right choices in all areas of living, because of my love for Him.

In intimacy with Him we discover the passion of His heart for a lost and dying world and we develop a burden for souls as we get His heart for the nations, while spending time in His presence.

> *"Take My yoke upon you and learn from Me, for I am gentle and lowly in heart, and you will find rest for your souls. For My yoke is easy and My burden is light."*
>
> *Matthew 11: 29-30*

8. Pray, Praise and Fast until the Vision is birthed

The power of prayer, praise and worship opens prison doors in our souls. Fasting added to it, breaks obstacles in the spirit realm and births forth the power anointing that destroys the yokes of bondage.

Esther knew the power of fasting that reveals divine strategy and brings breakthrough anointing.

Only by perseverance will we see fulfillment of the purposes and destiny of God in our lives!

5

The Anointing Oils and the Bridal attire

It is interesting to note that the preparation time for Esther to be brought before the king lasted twelve months. Twelve therefore, being the number of government, signifies the fullness of time. This time period, as seen throughout the Bible, varies in the life of each individual. We have to be ready and prepared for the "Kairos" time of God, which is the *appointed time* to be moved into our divine placement.

"...for thus were the days of their preparation apportioned: six months with oil of mryyh, and six months with perfumes and preparations for beautifying women."
Esther 1:12b

Six, being the number of man, signifies that the soul life must first be brought to death by a deep saturation in the oil of myrrh before we can be adorned with the perfumes and gifts of the Holy Spirit.

God knows in His governmental system how much time we need for our preparation as His Bride, but could this time period be "shortened" as we yield more fully to the Holy Spirit?

In the Book of Exodus, chapter 30, the Lord spoke to Moses and gave him the ingredients for the holy anointing oil with which the tabernacle and the ark of the Testimony was to be anointed.

The anointing does not come cheap; it has a high price! It is "smeared" by the Holy Spirit on and into those who have set themselves apart from this world for His purposes. They spend time at His feet, loving Him in obedience, adoring Him, worshipping Him from a heart that loves Him for Himself, not for His hand.

> *"Or do you not know that your body is the temple*
> *of the Holy Spirit who is in you,*
> *whom you have from God, and*
> *that you are not your own."*
> *1 Corinthians 6: 19*

The anointing is carried in consecrated vessels that have become a habitation for His glory! The holy anointing oil for the tabernacle and the ark of the Testimony was made up of five ingredients, namely **myrrh, sweet-smelling cinnamon, sweet-smelling cane, cassia and olive oil** (Exodus 30: 23-25).

It is noteworthy that half the time of Esther's preparation was taken up by the preparation with oil of *myrrh,* which speaks of **bitter suffering.**

i. Suffering

At the "cross" road of salvation the Bridal company receives myrrh as a prophetic gift to identify our lives with that of Christ. In the process of our preparation, the incense will go up as a fragrance to God while the gold is being formed on the inside.

Myrrh: (Hebrews **Mowr** "to drop").

Myrrh is made from the "tears" of the *Balsamodendron myrrha* tree. It is bitter in taste, but after it has been pulverized and burnt, it produces a sweet fragrance. The burning is also a very slow process.

A tree is symbolic of man, thus meaning the brokenness produced by man's bitter suffering, which produces a sweet disposition.

It is through the lacerations made in our very hearts through rejection, abuse, hatred, slander, loneliness and all kinds of oppression and persecution that the qualities of meekness, patience and longsuffering are produced.

Esther must have shed many tears for the loss of her parents and later on she had to leave everyone behind that she knew. She also had to submit to a totally different lifestyle, confined to the restrictions and limitations of life within the palace. Esther learned the valuable lesson that within your limitation lies your freedom. She made peace with her situation and instead of bitterness she developed grace, which shows in her sweet disposition and gave her favor in the king's court.

Suffering has many faces and forms, but if we can understand that it produces an anointing that brings authority, we can bear it by His grace and rejoice in it.

> *"My grace is sufficient for you, for My strength*
> *is made perfect in weakness.*
> *Therefore most gladly I will rather boast*
> *in my infirmities, that the power of Christ*
> *may rest upon me. Therefore I take pleasure*
> *in infirmities, in reproaches, in needs,*

> *in persecutions, in distresses, for Christ's sake.*
> *For when I am weak, then I am strong."*
> *2 Corinthians 12: 9-10*

Esther must have been very lonely in the secluded lifestyle that she had to adopt in her preparation for her destiny, but she submitted to the discipline of the Holy Spirit and remained sweet and gracious.

ii. Brokenness

It is the saturation in the oil of myrrh that strengthens us to choose the bitter cup of His will in our Gethsemanes.

> *"The sacrifices of God are a broken spirit*
> *A broken and contrite heart*
> *These, O God, You will not despise."*
> *Psalm 51: 17*

Suffering brings a wonderful opportunity to yield to the comfort of the Holy Spirit and be taught about His boundless grace. It drives us into the arms of our Beloved and He pours the balm of Gilead into our wounds. Often our "suffering" is produced by our own stubbornness to lay down our "rights and demands" through the willfulness of self.

When we are fully yielded to the Holy Spirit, His light shines into the secret places of attitudes and motives of the heart and convicts us of sin, righteousness and judgement.

> *"Godly sorrow produces repentance...*
> *what diligence it produced in you, what clearing*
> *of yourselves, what indignation, what fear,*
> *what vehement desire, what zeal,*
> *what vindication!"*
> *2 Corinthians 7: 10-11*

> *"If we confess our sins, He is faithful and just to forgive us our sins and to cleanse us from all unrighteousness."*
>
> *1 John 1: 9*

It is of utmost importance to keep our minds focused on Jesus in order to keep our joy and peace.

iii. Myrrh as an embalming Spice for the dead

Death of our old man brings the resurrection life of the Holy Spirit! Embrace the myrrh for the fragrance of the Christ life and crucify the flesh.

> *"I beseech you therefore, brethren, by the mercies of God, that you present your bodies a living sacrifice, holy, acceptable to God, which is your reasonable service."*
>
> *Romans 12: 1*

Oh, that we might recognize the fruit that comes from suffering and the privilege to be found worthy of having fellowship in the sufferings of Christ, being conformed to His death in order to *gain Christ and know Him and the power of His resurrection!*

> *"though He was a Son, yet He learned obedience through the things which He suffered."*
>
> *Hebrews 5: 8*

> *Let us receive the myrrh of suffering as an emblaming oil for the death of the old man so that it can never be resurrected again!*

The way to victory is to die to self!

Esther abandoned herself to God and entrusted herself fully into the care of the Holy Spirit to receive any discipline that came her way as needful preparation for the Bridegroom.

She embraced the myrrh with contentment.

> *"A bundle of myrrh is my Beloved to me*
> *That lies all night between my breasts."*
> *Song of Solomon 1: 13*

The Bride of Christ understands the abundance of Jesus' suffering on the cross in the dark night of the soul and finds comfort in her heart while pondering upon His victory on the cross. She is looking upon her pierced King (Zechariah 12:10) and she identifies with His suffering to be clothed with His glory.

> *"For I consider that the sufferings of this*
> *present time are not worthy to be compared*
> *with the glory which shall be revealed in us."*
> *Romans 8: 18*

> *"who for the joy that was set before Him endured the cross,*
> *despising the shame, and has sat down at the*
> *right hand of the throne of God."*
> *Hebrews 12: 2 (b)*

iv. The Garment of Salvation and the Robe of Righteousness

The secret of Christ as our Righteousness lies therein that, after confession of our sins, we must receive our forgiveness that was bought by the precious Blood of the Lamb and throw off the garbs of our own righteousness, which are like filthy rags. (Isaiah 64: 6)

At the same time we must live a life of forgiveness, releasing those who have sinned against us, while blessing our enemies. This is a secret of walking in the Spirit that releases peace and joy in our lives.

> "For the kingdom of God is not eating and drinking, but **righteousness** and **peace and joy** in the Holy Spirit."
> Romans 14: 17

> "I will greatly rejoice in the Lord
> My soul shall be joyful in my God;
> For he has clothed me with the
> **Garments of salvation**
> He has covered me with the
> **Robe of righteousness**
> As a **Bridegroom** decks himself with **ornaments**
> And as a **Bride** adorns herself with her **jewels**".
> Isaiah 61: 10

> "We are transformed by the renewing of our mind, that we may prove what is that good and acceptable and perfect will of God."
> Romans 12: 2

After repentance, we must see ourselves as righteous in

His Righteousness, wearing His *robe of righteousness* and *garments of salvation* like ornaments or jewels.

Isn't it wondrous how the Lord in His grace is not only stripping us of our sinful nature, but at the same time He is clothing us in splendor with the glorious garments of His Bride.

v. Fire precedes the Glory

Often we sing to the Lord, "send the fire," without realizing what we are asking for. When that fire comes in the form of suffering, testing or trial, we do not want to go through it, because we don't realize that the fire is a purifying agent in refining our character to pure gold.

> "…. For He is like a refiner's fire And like launderers' soap. He will sit as a refiner and a Purifier of silver; He will purify the sons of Levi And purge them as gold and silver, That they may offer to the Lord An offering in righteousness."
> Malachi 3: 2b – 3

The fire is a condition for the glory. When we yield to the baptism of fire, all the hay and stubble is burned out and our motives are purified to truly give God all the glory. In the process our characters become like purified gold, because God's glory is reflected in us.

Oh, may we embrace the fire that consumes self!

> "For our light affliction which is but for a moment, is working for us a far more exceeding and eternal weight of glory, while we do not look at the things which

are seen, but at the things which are not seen."
2 Corinthians 4: 17-18

"Beloved, do not think it strange concerning the fiery trial which is to try you, as though some strange thing happened to you; but rejoice to the extent that you partake of Christ's sufferings, that when His glory is revealed, you may also be glad with exceeding joy.
*If you are reproached for the name of Christ, blessed are you, **for the Spirit of glory and of God rests upon you.**"*
1 Peter 4: 12-14

When we have made a choice to be separated from the world to serve the King of kings and become His Bride, we can expect persecution.

We will not have the glory of the Lord without going through the suffering. The mountain of suffering, Calvary, draws us near – unto the mountain of glory, which is Zion, the presence of the Lord. In the process He heals our broken hearts, brings liberty to the captives and opens the prison doors.
He comforts us and consoles those who mourn.

"...to give them beauty for ashes..."
- Isaiah 61: 7b

Ashes are left only after the fire has consumed the sacrifice. This implies that our wolf nature has to be burned to ashes before we will receive the beauty of the Lamb's nature.

He gives us a **garment of praise** for a spirit of heaviness and *"oil of joy"* to rejoice in His victory on the cross.

vi. The Garment of Praise and the Oil of Joy for Mourning

Praise is like a garment – we have the choice to put it on! The Hebrew root for "garment" teaches us to literally "wrap" or "cover" ourselves with praise as with a warm coat. Praise is an antidote for depression, doubt, fear, loneliness and all negative emotions, but again it requires a sacrifice.

"Therefore by Him let us continually offer the sacrifice of praise to God, that is, the fruit of our lips, giving thanks to His name."
Hebrews 13: 15

If we learn to praise God in the face of seemingly insurmountable obstacles, He will surely give us the victory and make a way for us where there seems to be no way! Joy is a spiritual state, or in other words a condition of the human spirit, brought about by the Holy Spirit.

When we receive a revelation of the Bridegroom through the Holy Spirit, an unspeakable joy rises up in our spirits and we abound in thanksgiving. He has brought us out of Egypt into the Promised Land of His Kingdom of glory!

As we walk in the Spirit, keeping our mind focused on the Beloved and His Kingdom, singing His praises in our hearts; as we abide in His Word, meditating on it, day and night and acting upon it; and as we abide in His love, living a life of love towards Him and the brethern, our *joy* becomes full and our hearts overflow with His praises.

"In Your Presence is fullness of joy!"
- Psalm 16:11

> *"Awake, awake! Put on your strength*
> *Put on your beautiful garments*
> *Shake yourself from the dust, arise!"*
> *- Isaiah 52: 1*

The attitudes of our hearts determine the outcomes of our trials!

The attitudes and motives of the heart are changed in the furnace of affliction. Negative attitudes show hidden impurities that come to the surface in the melting pot. We have to get rid of our mumbling, grumbling and complaining, blaming others and God for our situations, else we will keep wandering in the wilderness around the same mountain and never enter the Promised Land of His glory.

We also have to confess our desire to be in control (because of fear) – manipulating, dominating and intimidating through our words and attitudes (which is witchcraft and gives way to the Jezebel spirit).

Everything of self has to be pulverized as incense to be burnt in His fire so that He can glorify it as a sweet aroma of worship. If we keep on concentrating on our suffering, we will smell of the smoke of the fire, but if we endure the heat of the fire, knowing that the Fourth Man is with us in it, putting all our faith and trust in Him as our Deliverer, our bondages will fall off and we will come out of the trial with a testimony of His victory! Our characters will be pure and refined – delivered of self - with the sweet fragrance of myrrh.

Embrace suffering for the aroma – dying brings you to the resurrection life of the Holy Spirit within and the position of being seated with Christ at the right hand of the Father in heavenly places (Ephesians 2: 6), exercising dominion over the forces of darkness by the anointing of His Name.

Self-pity and judgementalism will destroy you!
Until you can die to everything of self, you will not fulfill your purpose.

> *"My brethren, count it all joy when you fall into various trials, knowing that the testing of your faith produces patience. But let **patience** have its perfect work, that you may be perfect and complete, lacking nothing."*
> James 1: 2-4

We find it difficult to **rejoice** in trials and tribulations until we realize that good fruit comes after the pruning. In the process of the pruning, the tree "bleeds," but in a short time new growth is seen, fragrant blossoms appear and excellent fruit is produced. And isn't it true that only the unfruitful branches are cut off?

Knowing that the Vinedresser knows how to prune the branches to produce the best fruit, we can surrender to Him in full trust without fear and rejoice in His workmanship.

vii. Faith in the Fire

During the process of the fire our **faith** is purged from dross and stretched with undergirding **patience or longsuffering** to *wait* until the due time of God's deliverance. In this waiting we need to exercise **selfcontrol, which** produces **endurance** and **godliness.**

> *"But without faith it is impossible to please Him, for he who comes to God must believe that He is, and that He is*

a rewarder of those who diligently seek Him."
Hebrews 11: 6

Full surrender to God implies that we put our trust fully in Him, that we follow where He leads us and that our confession of His Lordship in our lives remains consistent.

Faith's worship of the Almighty God and a walk by the Holy Spirit's guidance does not depend on answered or unanswered prayers – it remains consistent in all circumstances.

Everyone who has ever walked out into the unknown future of God's call, had to step out on the water in faith and keep walking in faith,

*"looking unto Jesus,
the author and finisher of our faith....."*
Hebrews 12: 2

There will definitely be storms on the way, but He is the One who stills the storms when we call on Him; He is the One who takes your hand when the waves of your circumstances seem to overwhelm you and doubt and fear want to sink and drown you.

*"I love the Lord, because He has heard my voice
and my supplications,
Because He has inclined His ear to me,
Therefore I will call upon Him as long as I live."*
Psalm 116: 1-2

In the storm and in the wilderness the deepest impurities of the heart are revealed. He reveals to us our stubbornness, pride, unbelief, doubt and fears so that we can humble ourselves, lay it down on the altar and surrender our will to trust the Lord!

Don't die in the wilderness, go through in faith!

The water of the laver washes us as we saturate ourselves with the Word of God. We find direction and hope and our faith is strengthened by the promises of the Word.

Here we are trained, on our knees, to rule and reign together with the King in His Kingdom! Keep your eyes on the One who promised you the Promised Land!

"For what if some did not believe? Shall their unbelief make the faithfulness of God without effect? Certainly not! Indeed, let God be true but every man a liar."
Romans 3:3

"Therefore, having been justified by faith, we have peace with God through our Lord Jesus Christ, through whom also we have access by faith into this grace in which we stand, and rejoice in hope of the glory of God."
*"And not only that, but we also glory in tribulations, knowing that tribulation produces **perseverance**;*
*And perseverance, **character** And character, **hope**.*
*Now hope does not disappoint, because the **love** of God has been poured out in our hearts by the Holy Spirit who was given to us."*
Romans 5: 1-5

Faith thus brings us into the position where His **grace** abounds over us and makes us able to go through all the tests and trials "standing" and progressing through **perseverance**, to produce **character, hope and love.**

"....for by faith you stand."
2 Corinthians 1: 24 c

viii. Attitude in the waiting room

> *"For since the beginning of the world*
> *Men have not heard nor perceived by the ear*
> *Nor has the eye seen any God besides You*
> *Who acts for the one who waits for Him*
> ***You meet him who rejoices and***
> ***does righteousness***
> *Who remembers You in Your ways."*
> Isaiah 64: 4-5

Often we get impatient in the waiting room of God. We want it our way and we want our answers now. We want to by-pass the training ground that forms His character and we don't realize that our flesh cannot be clothed with His glory.

In His wisdom, God knows when the timing is right, and the sooner we make peace with that, the quicker we will grow into His image and the gold of His character will come forth from the inside.

Often we grow weary and tired while the refining process is going on, and the devil will even make us think that something is wrong with us, because it seems as if everyone else is just sailing through life without having to be washed with the launderer's soap.

We are inclined to give in to despondency, but if only we may realize that we are in a chosen position of His grace, like Esther, we will yield fully to the cleansing process, knowing that by His grace and lovingkindness He is transforming us into His glorious image.

While we're waiting, let us *rejoice* that He is sovereignly in control of our lives and every situation thereof.

> "Thanks be to God, who gives us
> the victory through Jesus Christ."
>
> 1 Corinthians 15: 57

Secondly, let my walk and talk and attitudes in relationship with God and men, be well pleasing in His sight, walking in righteousness.

Thirdly, let me remember that in all His ways, God is just and righteous and faithful – He will never let me down.

> "For He Himself has said, I will never leave you
> nor forsake you."
>
> Hebrews 13: 5b

ix. More Altars

> "I beseech you therefore brethren, by the mercies of God,
> that you present your bodies a living sacrifice, holy,
> acceptable to God, which is your reasonable service.
> And do not be conformed to this world, but be transformed
> by the renewing of your mind, that you may prove
> what is that good and acceptable
> and perfect will of God."
>
> Romans 12: 1-2

In times of tribulation and trial, build an altar for your fleshly reactions, reasoning, retaliations and the like and willingly yield to the Holy Spirit's fire to burn out your carnal nature in order to produce His fruit.

x. The Love Anointing

Embrace **love** as your weapon of warfare, as well as the shield over your heart.

"Let us who are of the day be sober,
putting on the breastplate of faith and love,
and as a helmet the hope of salvation."
1 Thessalonians 5:8

Putting on the breastplate of love will keep us from taking negative attitudes and unkind words from other people to heart. It will guard us against taking offense and help us to walk a walk of forgiveness in the love of Christ.

Loving God with all our heart, soul, mind and strength, will produce that perfect obedience that pleases His heart. Out of that will flow the love for our brothers and sisters in the faith, and to all people.

*"If you really fulfill the **royal law***
according to the Scripture,
*'**You shall love your neighbor as yourself**,'*
you do well."
James 2:8

This royal law, commanding us to love, is the king of all laws and it covers and fulfills all laws dealing with human relationships. Flow in the divine love-stream to bring healing and deliverance everywhere you go.

We also have to learn to be kind, which is **goodness** in action, sweetness of disposition, **gentleness** in dealing with others, benevolence, kindness, affability. All these attributes of character are part of love and are developed by crucifying the self life.

This is the principle thing we have to learn –
to love and to bless unconditionally.

*"This is My commandment that you love one
another as I have loved you. Greater love
has no one than this, than to lay down one's
life for his friends."*
John 15: 13

Esther was prepared by the anointing oils to be willing to lay down her life for her people.

If we have not love, we cannot come in union with Him as His Bride, because God is Love.

"Let us pursue love" (1 Corinthians 14: 1) ...and keep on looking into the mirror of 1 Corinthians 13, laying down the self that only seeks its own and allow the Holy Spirit to transform us into the image of the Bridegroom *"from glory to glory"* (2 Corinthians 3: 18).

*"If you keep My commandments, you will abide in My
love, just as I have kept my Father's commandments and
abide in His love. These things I have spoken to you,
that My joy may remain in you, and that your joy may be full."*
John 15: 11-12

It is more blessed to give than to receive and as we sow love, we reap love, and we are constantly filled with love, so that our walk becomes a love walk. Love is *the more excellent way.*

"Therefore, as the elect of God, holy and beloved, **put on**
(like garments) **tender mercies, kindness, humility,
meekness, longsuffering, bearing with one another,
and forgiving one another,** *if anyone has a complaint
against another, even as Christ forgave you,*

so you also must do.
***But above all these things put on love
which is the bond of perfection."***
Colossians 3: 12-14

*"By this all will know that you are My disciples,
if you have love for one another."*
John 13:35

If our motive for doing anything is not because of love for the Lord and our fellowmen, it will produce hay and stubble.

Esther developed such a sweet, loving character that *"she obtained favor in the sight of all who saw her."*
Esther 2: 15

*"If I have not love, I have become sounding
brass or a clanging cymbal."*
1 Corinthians 13: 1

We also have to overcome worry, stress and anxiety, that are by-products of the spirit of fear.

*"There is no fear in love;
but perfect love casts out fear,
because fear involves torment.
But he who fears has not been made perfect in Love"*
1 John 4: 18

*" ....do not worry about your life...
But seek first the kingdom of God and His righteousness,
and all these things shall be added to you".*
Matthew 6: 32-33

Esther had the eyes of her heart fixed on the Kingdom of God and the King of the Kingdom and because of her heart's attitude of worship, only seeking the desire of the King, she walked in the favor of His grace.

To worry, fume or fret is actually sin, because it shows that I do not trust God.

*"Be anxious for nothing, but in everything by prayer and supplication, with thanksgiving, let your requests be made known to God; and the **peace** of God, which surpasses all understanding, will guard your hearts and minds through Christ Jesus".*
Philippians 4: 6-7

When my mind is focused on the Lord Jesus and my heart is at rest, knowing that He is in control of my life, I will have perfect **peace.**

"You will keep him in perfect peace, whose mind is stayed on You, because he trusts in You."
Isaiah 26: 3

When our human reasoning cannot explain circumstances, we tend to doubt and fear and we want to take matters in our own hand. It is in these times that we can see whether our hearts are really **trusting** fully in the Lord and quietly following the instructions of the Holy Spirit.

"Now godliness with contentment is great gain".
2 Timothy 6: 6

Esther is a perfect example of **contentment** in her situation, which must have been very difficult for her, seeing that she was brought up in totally different surroundings with a different culture and different customs.

Everything was strange and new to her and she must have been very lonely, not having anyone around her that was familiar. Yet she was content to adapt to her situation without resisting the instructions of Mordecai and the prescriptions of Hegai. Because of her pleasing attitude, she found favor and was given the best place in the house (Esther 2: 9) with seven choice maidservants to assist her.

In His grace, God uses precious brothers and sisters in the body of Christ to assist us in our walk and growth in Him. They are the ones who would intercede for us, pray with us, encourage us, exhort us and even reprimand us in love when we are teachable and humble. It is by humility that we learn to appreciate the body of Christ.

God's **peace** is the blessed state of His rest in the security of His love that keeps our hearts and minds stable and surpasses all understanding.

If we look at the effect of the *anointing oil of myrrh*, we realize that suffering develops the **fruit of the Holy Spirit** in us and we are being clothed with royal garments.

The royal garments of the Bride can only be worn when we are disrobed of self.

An **exchange** has to take place. We have to **take off** the old man and **put on Christ!**

Fleshly Garments	Bridal Garments
Our Righteousness	Robe of His righteousness
Wickedness	Garments of salvation
Despondency, heaviness	Garment of Praise
Pride	Apron of humility
Unkindness	Tender mercies, goodness
Impatience	Longsuffering, patience perseverance
Lies	Girdle of Truth
Ungodliness	Holiness
Selfishness, hate, fear	Breastplate of faith and love

These garments speak of our outward attitudes and behavior – our outward appearance. Together with our beautiful new garments we also put on the **"whole armor of God"** which protects us against the principalities, powers, rulers of darkness, spiritual hosts of wickedness in the heavenly places and makes us able to withstand in the evil day, and having done all, to stand:

*"Stand therefore, having girded your waist with **truth**, having put on the breastplate of **righteousness**, and having shod your feet with the preparation of the gospel of **peace**; above all, taking up the shield of **faith**, with which you will be able to quench*

> *all the fiery darts of the wicked one,*
> *And take the **helmet of salvation** and*
> *The sword of the Spirit, which is the **Word of God**;*
> ***Praying always** with all prayer and supplication*
> *In the Spirit, being watchful to this end with*
> *all perseverance and supplication for all the saints."*
> *Ephesians 6: 14-18*

We now have **new garments, God's armor** and the **oil of JOY and gladness.**

We have received the HOLY SPIRIT and walk on the highway of Holiness (Isaiah 35), perfecting holiness in the fear of God.

We are reminded that without suffering we will not see the glory of His image in us.

> *"The Spirit itself bears witness with*
> *our spirit that we are the children of God,*
> *and if children, then heirs, heirs of God*
> *and joint heirs with Christ, if so be*
> *that we suffer with Him*
> *that we may also be glorified together."*
> *Romans 8:16 - 17*

We are told to *put on* the new garments and the armor of God, but **we** cannot put His glory on us. This is being worked by the Holy Spirit from the inside out as our characters are refined to pure gold within.

> *"And the glory which You gave me*
> *I have given them,*
> *that they may be one*
> *just as We are one."*
> *John 17: 22*

One day we will realize that the glory of the Lord is shining over us. We do not know when it became visible, but we know it happened some time when we stopped trying to take His glory for ourselves for the works He has done.

"Arise, shine;
For your light has come!
And the glory of the Lord is
Risen upon you!"
Isaiah 60: 1

The Bridal garments and the battle armor are kept in place by a constant washing of the Word of God, while we are bathed in prayer and worship.

6

Time and Timing in the waiting room.

Time (**Kairos**): (Strong's #2540): "Opportune time, set time, appointed time, due time, definite time, seasonable time, proper time for action."

It is crucial that we will know God's timing. If we move out in our impatience and hastiness, our mission and vision will fail and we will produce an Ishmael. If we wait too long, we'll miss it! We have to discern the season that we are in.

Take time to minister love songs to the Lord while the Shepherd is leading you beside the still waters of the river, feeding you in the green pastures with His life and love, where you learn to know Him and all His attributes by the Holy Spirit.

Wait (**Qavah**): (Strong's #6960): "to bind together by twisting."

This is the opportunity to get intertwined with Him in intimate fellowship, like the strings in a rope twisted together.

Do not be moved by other people's pressure and by what

they think you should do to be *busy*. Business with many works, like Martha, will make you miss the blessings at the feet of the Master.

> *"But Martha was distracted with much serving, and she approached Him and said, "Lord, do You not care that my sister has left me to serve alone? Therefore tell her to help me." And Jesus answered and said to her, "Martha, Martha, you are worried and troubled about many things. But one thing is needed, and Mary has chosen that good part, which will not be taken away from her."*
> Luke 10: 40-42

Crucify that Martha in you that accuses you of being lazy and slothful, who wants to keep you busy with many distractions in the fleshly realm. Spend time with the Holy Spirit in the inner chamber where He instructs you about the things that are pleasing in the sight of the King to only do the assignments of the Holy Spirit.

> *"There is now no condemnation to those who are in Christ Jesus, who do not walk according to the flesh, but according to the Spirit."*
> Romans 8: 1

Often we think we are ready for His calling when only half of the preparation is done and we create Ishmaels by our own impatience to wait on God's timing. After we have gone through some suffering, and we recognize that the Holy Spirit has begun a good work in us, we want to plunge into works, but now further anointing oils need to be administered.

We have to be *patient* until the fire has consumed the offering of sacrifice or else we will not stand the test that purity requires.

Put your trust fully in Him. While David was faithfully tending the sheep in the field, singing love songs to the Lord on his harp, God had already instructed Samuel to anoint him as king. Yet he had to spend many years in caves, fleeing from his enemies before he could step into his appointed office.

During this time of waiting on God's timing, he never ceased worshipping God while remaining faithful.

Negative circumstances often cause us to think that all is lost and that God's promises are never going to be fulfilled, but this is the time to keep our eyes on the Lord and worship Him in spirit and in truth!

Like Moses, Abraham, Joseph, David and many others, let us remain faithful in our daily walk, living the kingdom life as worshippers of the King, waiting with patience and full trust for His perfect timing.

Esther waited with patience until her appointed time came to be brought before the king and she was content to wait until Hegai decided to call her.

When the time is ripe for you to rise up to your destiny, God will not be asleep! The Holy Spirit is constantly watching over you and will alert you at the right time and you will know that it is He, opening the doors before you to step out into a higher place in your calling.

Wait and listen for the strategy of the season!

7

More Ingredients of the Anointing Oils

In our quest for God, we have progressed from the place of natural light in the Outer Court into the Holy Place; from the place of original surrender to the light of His lampstand, the table of His shewbread and the altar of incense.

The Holy Place signifies the place where the soul life must be sanctified. The seven-branched lampstand provides light in the Holy Place where our natural mind is illuminated by the seven-fold Spirit of the Lord (Isaiah 11) as we study His Word. The lampstand was made of beaten gold, which signifies the forming and shaping of our carnal mind patterns as we are enlightened by the Holy Spirit through revelation knowledge.

> *"Your Word is a lamp to my feet and a light to my path"*
>
> Psalm 119: 105

At the table of unleavened shewbread, our wills are finely ground, as the flour for the bread. Our stubbornness, willfulness and our "rights" are surrendered to the Lordship of Jesus in order to yield to His will in all situations.

> *"Then Jesus said to those Jews who believed Him,*
> *If you abide in My word, you are My disciples indeed.*
> *And you shall know the truth, and the truth*
> *shall make you free."*
>
> John 8: 32

Our adoration for the King is increasing daily as we meditate on His Word and grow in the knowledge of our Beloved.

In this process of sanctification, more of the ingredients of the anointing oil become noticeable in our character through the sweet fragrance that is given off.

Sweet-smelling Cinnamon:

This is derived from the aromatic **inner rind** of the *Laurus cinnamomum*. It has a delightful odor when burning and speaks of *a holy,* **separated walk before the Lord.**

> *"A garden enclosed*
> *I my sister, my spouse,*
> *A spring shut up, a fountain sealed"*
>
> Song of Solomon 4: 12

The walk of the Bride is on a highway of holiness (Isaiah 35) and she is set apart, and fully surrendered to the Holy Spirit to live a holy life, fully consecrated to the Lord.

> *"Pursue peace with all people,*
> *and holiness, without which*
> *no one will see the Lord."*
>
> Hebrews 12:14

As we spend time in the closet in separation, gazing into the beauty of His holiness while we meditate on the Word, we are constantly being transformed through repentance, and sanctified by the truth (John 17:17, 19).

Sweet-smelling Cane:

Cane is a reed-like grass that grows along streams. It denotes the **sweetness of the disposition** that is derived from drinking of the river of Life. It also conveys the idea of **uprightness.**

Being saturated with the Word of God, fills us with His sweet Spirit and the words that we speak bring grace to the hearer.

> *"Pleasant words are like a honeycomb,*
> *Sweetness to the soul and*
> *Health to the bones."*
> *Proverbs 16:24*

Our garments have been scented with myrrh, but now they need the scent of cassia.

> *"All Your garments are scented with myrrh,*
> *and aloes and cassia."*
> *Psalm 45: 8*

Cassia:

The **inner** bark of an aromatic plant native to SE Asia used as a source of cinnamon. It is a spice for the banqueting table where we entertain the King.

Cassia stands for a ***humble bowing down, to do homage, worship, adore, revering Him in the fear of God.***

Jesus is not there to just answer our needs, but to be worshipped for who He is. This spice brings an ***anointing of humility.***

"Learn from Me, for I am meek and lowly in heart."
Matthew 11: 29

Esther submitted to Mordecai in **meekness**, without rebellion and stayed in that same attitude of **lowliness**, and with a **gentle** spirit also submitted to Hegai.

The Bible teaches us that the tree is known by its fruit. Esther humbly accepted whatever was prescribed to her by the Holy Spirit.

If we do not humble ourselves, we will be humiliated!

In the process, we also become His handmaidens who would be willing to serve with the apron of humility.

"Likewise you younger people, submit yourselves to your elders.
Yes, all of you be submissive to one another, and
*be clothed with **humility**, for*
God resists the proud,
*But gives grace to **the humble**.*
Therefore humble yourselves under the mighty hand of God,
that He may exalt you in due time,
Casting all your care upon Him, for He cares for you".
1 Peter 5: 5 - 7

Here we see that the way up is down. The proud will not see God's glory – God will resist them!

We learn to delight ourselves in Him, the Beloved and our seeking is not after the gifts anymore, but after the Giver.

In this partial light though, there is still duality between the spirit and the carnal mind because of the reasoning in our hearts, together with murmuring and complaining. The Holy Spirit will drop something into our spirits and seconds later our minds will start reasoning and analyzing the information and confusion sets in.

The spiritual heart consists of the conscience (the leading part of the spirit), our mind, our emotion and our will. It is like the central station between the soul and the spirit and receives input from both.

The direction in which the heart is turned, is indicative of its condition. If the heart is divided between the desires of the flesh on the one hand and on the other hand it yearns for the things of the Spirit, there will be frustration and turmoil.

"...whenever their hearts turn to the Lord, the veil is taken away. And the Lord is the Spirit; and where the Spirit of the Lord is, there is freedom."
2 Corinthians 3:16-17

Olive oil:

This is derived from the crushing of olives and is symbolic of surrender to the **Holy Spirit.**

Nothing of eternal value will ever be accomplished by the power of self.

"Not by might, nor by power, but by My Spirit, says the Lord of hosts."
Zechariah 4: 6

This is also the *pure* oil that was used for the golden lampstand in the temple that burned continuously (Exodus 27: 20). The Holy Spirit brings the illumination of the Word into our hearts so that our hearts can be set aflame with zeal for the house of God and our light can shine continuously as we are being filled with the Holy Spirit.

The anointing of the Holy Spirit teaches us to abide in Christ and empowers us for the great commission to do the work of the ministry. He endows us with His gifts for the edifying of the body of Christ.

"But the anointing which you have received from Him
abides in you, and you do not need that anyone teach you;
but as the same anointing teaches you concerning all things, and
is true, and not a lie, and just as it has taught you,
you will abide in Him."

1 John 2: 2

8

Scent for Our Garments

In the garden of the bride of Solomon there are pleasant fruits, grown for the delight of the bridegroom.

> *"Your plants are an orchard of **pomegranates**
> with pleasant fruits,
> fragrant **henna**, with **spikenard**,
> spikenard and **saffron**,
> **calamus** and **cinnamon**,
> with all trees of **frankincense**,
> **myrrh** and **aloes**
> with all the chief spices."*
> Song of Solomon 4: 13-14

These fruits are produced when we drink of the river of life (Ezekiel 47: 12).

Pomegranates:

This fruit, when cut, displays rows of red "pips" which speak of **pure and loving thoughts,** *a mind washed by the blood of the Lamb,* filled with love and adoration for the Beloved.

Henna produces a *red dye* that was used by the Oriental brides to spread on the palms of their hands and on their feet on the night before the wedding. This signifies the **Blood of our Lord Jesus Christ**, cleansing us from all unrighteousness so that we can lift up holy hands before the Lord and walk before Him in uprightness and holiness.

> *"Who may ascend into the hill of the Lord?*
> *Or who may stand in His holy place?*
> *he who has **clean hands** and a **pure heart***
> *who has not lifted up his soul to an idol*
> *nor sworn deceitfully."*
>
> Psalm 24: 3-4

We need to be sensitive and repent instantly when we detect anything that might have grieved the Holy Spirit and receive the cleansing of the Blood of Jesus.

Spikenard:

This signifies **light** which is spread through the fragrance of our worship that shows our love, appreciation and dedication to Him.

Jesus Christ is our Light that lights us up from the inside.

> *"In Your light, we see light."*
>
> Psalm 36:9b

If there is any area in our thought life where we allow negativity, we allow darkness to creep in and we are not walking in the light. This will show in our reactions, speech, choices and attitudes and will affect our relationships with others.

> *"But if we walk in the light*
> *as He is in the light,*
> *we have fellowship with one another,*
> *and the blood of Jesus Christ His Son*
> *cleanses us from all sin."*
>
> 1 John 1: 7

Esther was like a shining light in the king's chambers and it brought her great favor wherever she went. This was shown by her acts and conduct in righteousness, charity and goodness before the Lord and resulted in good relationships.

Saffron:

Of the *Iris* order, it is esteemed for its fragrance and medicinal value and denotes **godliness.**

> *"...but **godliness** is profitable for all things,*
> *having promise of the life that now is*
> *and of that which is to come."*
> 1 Timothy 4: 8

We are commanded to diligently add to our faith virtue, knowledge, self-control, perseverance, **godliness**, brotherly kindness and brotherly love.

Calamus:

This comes from an aromatic cane which grows like stalks and signifies an **upright** life.

> *"the generation of the upright will be blessed."*
> Psalm 112: 2b

> *"Unto the upright there arises light in the darkness;*
> *he is gracious and full of compassion,*
> *and righteous."*
>
> Psalm 112: 4

Cinnamon:

We have seen that the oil that comes from this fruit is an ingredient of the anointing oil because of its sweet smell unto the Lord.

This fruit is found in the King's **private** garden - for Him to delight in its fragrant odor. It denotes the life in the **inner chamber of prayer and worship** and is very precious to the Lord.

When we walk in a **separated, consecrated** lifestyle, it produces a sweet-smelling fragrance in God's nostrils.

> *""For we are to God the fragrance of Christ*
> *among those who are being saved*
> *and among those who are perishing."*
>
> 2 Corinthians 2:15

The third aspect of the soul, namely the emotional life, is dealt with at the altar of incense. This is the place where all the emotions of my heart are finally surrendered to the Lordship of Jesus. The four-square facet of the altar signifies a balanced emotional life where this aspect of my soul life is poured out in worship to the Holy One.

The horns of the altar signify strength, and so my natural strength is part of the sacrifice that brings me into the higher realm of the Spirit. At this altar our lives are given over to Him as a living sacrifice of worship and adoration to the King of kings and Lord of lords. We are stepping over into the life of the Spirit within the veil.

9

ಖ಼ಖ಼

The Altar of Incense

The Altar of Incense is the decisive point. This is where the carnal mind has to be sacrificed on the altar of worship, my will is subjected to God's will, my emotions are brought in subjection to the Spirit of Life and my heart is **totally** focused on the Lord Jesus Christ and what he has accomplished for me on Calvary.

> *"There is now no condemnation to those who are*
> *in Christ Jesus, who do not walk according to the flesh,*
> *but according to the Spirit.*
> *For the law of the Spirit of life has freed me*
> *in Christ Jesus from the law of sin and death."*
> Romans 8: 1-2

Now we put on our **priestly garments** to minister to the Holy One, sweet fragrances in golden bowls full of incense burnt on the altar.

> *"And the Lord said to Moses: Take **sweet spices, stacte,***
> ***onycha and galbanum and pure frankincense***
> *with these sweet spices; there shall be equal amounts of each."*
> *"You shall make of these an incense, a compound*

> *according to the art of the perfumer, salted, pure and holy."*
> *"And you shall beat some of it very fine*
> *and put some of it before the Testimony*
> *in the tabernacle of meeting where I will meet*
> *with you. It shall be most holy to you."*
>
> Exodus 30: 34–36

Stacte: (**stazoo** "to drop")

This ingredient comes from a tree, *Storax Officinale.* The tears of gum "drops" from the bark and denotes *walking in grace and truth* like Jesus (John.1:12). It signifies a life that is "poured out" for the King.

As we have received mercy and grace, we ought to be merciful and gracious in our words and deeds. Only when we realize how much the Lord has done for us, can we extend His mercy and grace to the people around us.

> *"for He makes His sun rise on the evil*
> *and on the good, and*
> *sends rain on the just and on the unjust."*
>
> Matthew 5: 45b

Onycha: (a shell or a scale, the horny cap of a shell).

It is used for compounding perfume. It is both a perfume and a medicine and odorous because the shell fish feed on nard.

It denotes **boldness** to come to the throne of God, and *boldness* to witness to a lost and dying world.

To have this boldness, we cannot walk in fear or in condemnation.

> *"Therefore brethren, having boldness to enter the*

Holiest by the blood of Jesus..."

Hebrews 10: 17

It is also part of our equipment which we receive in the secret place to come against the enemy of our souls in spiritual warfare.

Galbanum: (Chelbenah)

"bleeds" from a tree trunk as a milky substance in small round tears that changes into a gum resin. When mixed with fragrant substances, it has the effect of increasing the odor and making it last longer. It speaks of **"plenty"** or **"increase."**

Our worship should be an extravagant abandonment to the Lord, sparing nothing - not being ashamed of an open display of our affections.

"Oh, worship the Lord in the beauty of holiness!"

Psalm 96: 9

"worshipping God in Spirit and in Truth"

(John 4:24)

Frankincense:

A gum resin from the *Boswellia tree*, white in color and burning with a white flame. (**Lebonah** from **laban** *"to be white"*).

"*Frank* – 1. open and honest in expressing what one thinks or feels; candid. 2. free from disguise or guile."

The white color represents **purity**.

"Blessed are the **pure** in heart, for they shall see God."

Matthew 5: 8

The white flame represents a **pure conscience.** We can not compromise with sin in any form or degree.

Frankincense is a fruit in the enclosed garden of the King, as well as an ingredient of the incense.

Purity and truth in the heart are also requirements for those who may abide in His tabernacle and may dwell in His holy hill (Psalm 15). This brings us in fellowship with the Godhead.

It is significant that all these substances for the incense had to be crushed and pulverized to fine powder, then compounded and salted. All these substances are bitter in taste but produce a sweet fragrance when burned. Salt is for preservation.

On this altar we offer the brokenness of our selfish human nature, which is bitter to our taste, but when offered to the Lord in honest, humble surrender, openly free from disguise or guile, it becomes a sweet fragrance of worship in His nostrils.

Our praises and prayers are a worship offering (Revelation 5: 8). Here we get enveloped in the smoke of the incense and we step through the veil in full assurance of faith that He meets with us here at the mercy seat, which is the throne of grace.

"Therefore, brethren, having boldness
to enter the Holiest by the blood of Jesus
by a new and living way which He consecrated for us,
through the veil, that is His flesh,
and having a High Priest over the house of God,
Let us draw near with a true heart
In full assurance of faith, Having our hearts sprinkled
From an evil conscience and our bodies
washed with pure water."
Hebrews 10: 19 - 22

During her preparation time, Esther had to learn how to come to the mercy seat to obtain grace in time of need.

Our prayers are kept in heaven as incense in golden bowls and the twenty-four elders sing a new song, saying:

"You are worthy to take the scroll,
And to open its seals; For You were slain,
And have redeemed us to God by Your Blood out of every tribe
and tongue and people and nation
*And have made us **kings and priests to our God***
And we shall reign on earth."
Revelation 5: 9 – 10

*"But you are a chosen generation, a **royal priesthood**,*
a holy nation, His own special people, that you may
proclaim the praises of Him who called you out of
darkness into His marvelous light; who once were not a people,
but are now the people of God, who had not obtained mercy
but now have obtained mercy."
1 Peter 2: 9 – 10

As we bring our offering of worship, praise and thanksgiving before the Lord, pouring out our hearts to Him in bold, pure, extravagant worship, the faculties of our soul life are taken up in Him and aligned with His mind, will and emotions. This brings us right into the throne room of His Presence, carrying the fragrance with us.

10

The Bridal Tent

> "Esther requested nothing but what Hegai the King's eunuch, the custodian of the women, advised. And Esther obtained favor in the sight of all who saw her. So Esther was taken to King Ahasuerus, into his royal palace. The king loved Esther more than all the other women, and she obtained grace and favor in his sight more than all the virgins; so he set the royal crown upon her head and made her queen instead of Vashti."
>
> Esther 2:15b-17

1. Kingly Anointing

When Esther was brought before the king, she was already made beautiful by the inner adornments of the Spirit – she came in humility and simplicity with no "adornments" of the flesh to impress Him – no name, no reputation, no qualifications or achievements; no agenda other than to please Him.

> "Do not let your adornment be **merely outward** – arranging the hair, wearing gold or putting on fine apparel –

*rather let it be the **hidden person of the heart, with the incorruptible beauty of a gentle and quiet spirit,** which is very precious in the sight of God."*
1 Peter 3: 3-4

Her *chaste conduct in submissiveness* won the King's heart and the favor of his grace.

When we reach the point where we want nothing for ourselves and our motives are pure, we eagerly yield to the Holy Spirit that God can be glorified.

Now God, who knows the intents and purposes of the heart, can entrust us with His authority by His grace and favor.

*"And You have **crowned** him with glory and honor."*
Psalm 8: 5b

He has crowned us with His glory and honor and we have stepped into the kingly anointing, ruling and reigning with Christ Jesus.

"(He) has raised us up together, and made us sit together in the heavenly places in Christ Jesus."
Ephesians 2: 6

In heavenly places this calls for a feast of celebration when we take our place in Christ Jesus.

"Then the king made a great feast, the Feast of Esther, for all his officials and servants; and he proclaimed a holiday in the provinces and gave gifts according to the generosity of a king."
Esther 2: 18

From this position we are given the authority to be sent out on assignment by the King in the Apostolic anointing.

2. Intimacy

> "All Thy garments are scented with **myrrh**
> and **aloes and cassia**,
> Out of the ivory palaces, by which
> they have made You glad...
> So the King will greatly desire your beauty;
> Because He is your Lord, Worship Him"
> Psalm 45: 8, 11

Myrrh:

Our **persecution and suffering** for the Name of Christ has now become an aroma of His glory. At last we realize that this is something to rejoice in greatly because it makes us partakers of His glory. Myrrh endows us with grace.

> "For I consider that the sufferings of this
> present time are not worthy to be
> compared with the glory that
> shall be revealed in us."
> Romans 8: 18

At first we complained when going through suffering, but now it has become a perfume for our garments which is part of our fellowship with Christ and it becomes a beautiful fragrance unto Him. Myrrh endows us with grace and sweetness.

> "For to you it has been granted on behalf
> of Christ, not only to believe in Him,
> but also to suffer for His sake."
> Philippians 1: 29

When the heart moves in union with God, we are moved from positional authority to intimacy.

Aloes : (Ahalim)

The perfume is from the oil thickening into resin **within the trunk and used for perfuming garments and beds. It signifies the *place of intimacy with the Beloved.***

The leaves of the plant are crushed and the juice is used for detoxifying, cleansing and healing purposes. The beginning of worship is the experience of the forgiveness of our sins.

> *"If we say that we do not have sin,*
> *We are deceiving ourselves,*
> *And the truth is not in us.*
> *If we confess our sins, He is faithful*
> *and righteous to forgive us our sins*
> *and cleanse us from all unrighteousness."*
> *1 John 1: 8-9*

The veil was torn when Jesus yielded up His Spirit (Matthew 27: 57) and through His shed, holy blood He consecrated the living way for us through the veil, that is His Flesh. This means that He paid the price that we can have victory over our flesh through identification with His death and resurrection and live the victorious life beyond the veil through His Spirit.

I have walked through the veil of separation into His Presence, singing love songs of worship to my Beloved, having fully received the finished work on the cross. The New Testament of His blood covenant has made me joint heir with Christ in the Resurrection Life. His favor abounds over me because I have answered the call of His heart to have communion with Him.

I have the eyes of my heart fully focused on Him, worshipping Him in Spirit and in Truth, my inner being totally filled with love for Him.

My worship becomes personal in an intimate communicative relationship. A divine romance is flowing between the Bridegroom and the Bride.

This anointing oil has healing properties and has been poured out over me like the balm of Gilead while worshipping the Beloved in a total abandonment of my whole being to His Love. It releases the fragrance of the Beloved. (2 Corinthians 2:14) In the security of the Father's love I find rest and peace. He has provided all that I will ever need in the sacrifice of His Son. I am delivered of all fear and doubt in the intimacy of His Love and I can put my trust wholly in Him as I worship Him as my Maker and my Husband, my Redeemer, my Friend, my Shepherd, my Waymaker, my Provider, my Healer and Deliverer and everything else that I may have need of.

He has become reality to me and His love is constantly cleansing me from all hidden impurities.

> "I am my Beloved's And my Beloved is mine.."
> - Song of Solomon 6: 3

> "Behold, you are fair, my love!
> Behold you are fair! You have dove's eyes"
> - Song of Songs 1:15

Cassia: **(Quddah)** As we move into a higher dimension of worshipping God, we **bow down lower** because our revelation of His greatness becomes deeper.

> *The higher the exaltation of God, the deeper shall be our bow before Him!*

Now we will not need to talk about worshipping Him, our lives will be an altar of worship and our garments (conduct) will be drenched in the perfume of worship to Him alone.

> *"Exalt the Lord our God,*
> *and worship at His footstool –*
> *He is holy."*
>
> Psalm 99: 5

The veil has been lifted from our eyes through the new covenant of His Blood. We have entered the realm of Unapproachable light and now we

3. *Behold the Lamb!*

The psalmist describes the Messiah and His Bride:

> *"You are fairer than the sons of men;*
> *Grace is poured upon Your lips;*
> *Therefore God has blessed You forever.*
> *Gird Your sword upon Your thigh, O Mighty One*
> *With Your glory and Your majesty.*
> *And in Your majesty ride prosperously because of*
> *Trust, humility, and righteousness;*
> *And Your right hand shall teach You awesome things.*
> *Your arrows are sharp in the heart of the King's enemies;*
> *The peoples fall under You*

Your throne, O God, is forever and ever;
A scepter of righteousness is the scepter of Your kingdom.
You love righteousness and hate wickedness;
Therefore God, Your God, has anointed You
With the oil of gladness more than Your companions.
All Your garments are scented
With myrrh and aloes and cassia
Out of the ivory palaces, by which
They have made You glad.
King's daughters are among Your honorable women;
At Your right hand stands the
Queen in gold from Ophir.
Listen, O daughter,
Consider and incline your ear;
Forget your own people also, and
Your father's house;
So the King will greatly desire your beauty;
Because He is your Lord, worship Him
The royal daughter is all glorious
Within the palace;
Her clothing is woven with gold.
She shall be brought to the King
in robes of many colors;
The virgins, her companions, who follow her,
shall be brought to You.
With gladness and rejoicing they shall be brought
They shall enter the King's palace.
Psalm 45: 2-15

In the Holy of Holies we behold Him and we become totally undone. We look into the beauty of His holiness and we abandon ourselves in holy adoration, pouring out our alabaster vases of love oil over His feet, unashamedly lovesick for our Beloved.

Intimate love talk is exchanged between the Bridegroom and the Bride. We hear His every whisper of love as our ears are tuned to His voice.

We know the comfort of His embraces as we are absorbed in Him and the desire of the Bride is:

"Let Him kiss me with the kisses of His mouth..."
Song of Solomon 1:2

What is this kiss? It is the kiss of the Word or the kiss of the Torah or the kiss of revelation.

The application of the Divine Kiss to the soul takes place where the Living Word is received and implanted into the humble heart as a seed of life to bring forth the fruit. In intimate fellowship, where my heart is joined to His, He"kisses" me with a personal Word of His mouth as He whispers His Word into my spirit.

I, in turn, return His kisses by agreeing with His Word by praising Him with His own Word in faith. I then prophesy His Word into my life and rejoice in His love. Divine communion takes place.

4. The Realm of His Glory

"The King has brought me into His chambers
We will be glad and rejoice in You

> *We will remember your love more than wine."*
> Song of Songs 1:4

As we worship Him in the beauty of His holiness, our praises go up as incense in a sweet fragrance to the Lord to come down over us in a canopy of grace that covers us and tabernacles over us within the cloud of His glory.

> *"But we all with unveiled face, beholding*
> *and reflecting like a mirror the glory of the Lord,*
> *are being transformed into the same image*
> *from glory to glory,*
> *even as from the Lord Spirit."*
> 2 Corinthians 3:16-18

He saturates us with the elements of who He is. Thus we are in an ongoing process being transformed to have His life, by the power of His life-giving Spirit with His Life essence. We are being transfigured, by the renewing of our mind, into His image.

There is a continuing process of deliverance, healing, restoration and refreshing going on in the Glory Cloud – in our spirit, soul, mind, body and circumstances of life.

This is an ongoing process in the resurrection life proceeding from the Spirit – *"from glory to glory!"*

To behold the glory of the Lord is to look into His very being and know His character, His mind, His heart, and His emotions. To reflect the glory of the Lord is to enable others to see Him through us by living Him.

The Holy Spirit ministers life to us in order that we can be ministers of that same life in Christ Jesus. This is a ministry in glory (2 Corinthians 3: 8).

He dwells in us as the Spirit of life (2 Corinthians 3: 6), we have become His habitation – to make Himself and all that He has accomplished, obtained and attained a reality to us, that we may be one with Him and be transformed into the same image as the Lord, the resurrected and glorified Christ, (2 Corinthians 3: 18).

He imparts the divine life into us, making us ministers of the Covenant of Life.

In this glory realm the Holy Spirit is **inscribing** the laws of Christ's love onto the tablets of our hearts of flesh as living letters with Christ as the content to convey and express Christ Jesus as Lord. Here, the "hidden manna" is given to the Bride and she is eating from "the tree of life."

This is the proper new covenant ministry where the life-giving Spirit writes His love message first in the hearts of those who minister to Him and then in the hearts of those that receive ministry from them.

We cannot minister in the "outer court" before we have ministered our love and adoration to the Lord in the face of His glory in the "inner court," the Holy of Holies. This is where His life-giving Spirit inscribes His heart on our hearts and clothes us with His glory.

> *"For if there is glory with the ministry of condemnation, much more the ministry of righteousness abounds with glory".*
> *2 Corinthians 3: 9*

Our lifestyles will be the sermon that will be read and His glorious life in us will draw people to Jesus as He is lifted up.

The ministry of the New Covenant is a ministry of the

Spirit through righteousness unto life. The Spirit is the life supply and righteousness, the living out and expression of Christ, who as the Spirit is our Life.

Now we are within the cloud, not to move out of His Presence back and forth, but to abide in Him as He abides in us (John 15).

His power is constantly at work in our inner being and we are being saturated with Him through a constant yielding to His Spirit. Now we come to know the riches of the glory of God's mystery among the Gentiles:

"Christ in you, the hope of glory!"
Colossians 1: 27

The more we turn our thoughts inward, focusing on Christ, our Beloved, loving Him, adoring Him, communing with Him, the more we will grow in that oneness with the Father and the Son, through the Holy Spirit.

The process to come in union with the Trinity is a matter of growth in the grace and knowledge of our Lord and Savior, Jesus Christ (II Peter 3:18).

All our reactions to the outer world must proceed from within, out of the realm of glory. We worship Him in the beauty of His holiness and suddenly we see our own unholiness like Isaiah. (Isaiah 6: 5) As we repent and confess our sins, He sanctifies every motive and content of our hearts by sending the fire on our offering.

All our self-righteousness, pride, opinions and judgments fall off and we see ourselves for what we really are. The religious cloak falls off and we see our selfishness, false piety and facades of pretense. This Light is blinding our natural eyesight and we see our nakedness in the True Light of Jesus. Here we deal with our carnality and even our intents and motives are searched to walk in the light and truth of the revelation of His Life.

Obedience spells death to self through humble repentance, but it brings grace and life. The great "I Am" manifests Himself when the "I" of self is in the grave. As we look into His glory, we are filled with His light and become reflectors of His light.

Our one desire is now to be one with Him. All the faculties of the soul, namely the mind, will and emotions must come in union with the Trinity. Eventually, the soul loses its existence in God, spiritually speaking, through a loving and perfect sinking of the soul into Him. His desires are our desires, His will is our will, His heart is our heart. He saturates us with His Love to love like He does. We become lovesick for the Beloved. He is our breath, our life, and our reason for living. We abide in Him as He in us, in His Word and in His Love. We bear the fruit of the Spirit in fullness and our joy is full (John 15).

Here we discover perfect peace because the Prince of peace has become our peace. We become peacemakers and enter into His rest.

> *"He keeps him in perfect peace whose mind is stayed on Him."*
>
> Isaiah 26: 3

Our minds must stay focused on the finished work of the Cross of Christ Jesus.

Any negative thought "sentence" or thought "picture" that enters our mind must be cast down in the name and by the blood of Jesus.

> *"For the weapons of our warfare are not carnal*
> *but mighty in God for pulling down*
> *of strongholds, casting down arguments*
> *and every high thing that exalts itself*
> *against the knowledge of God,*
> *bringing every thought into captivity to the*
> *obedience of Christ, and being ready*
> *to punish all disobedience*
> *when your obedience is fulfilled".*
> 2 Corinthians 10:4-6

At the same time our eyes must stay fixed on Jesus.

> *"…looking away unto Jesus the Author and*
> *Perfecter of our faith."*
> Hebrews 12: 2a

This implies that we should look away from anything that can distract our attention from beholding our Lord.

> *"For David says concerning Him:*
> *I foresaw the Lord always before my face,*
> *For He is at my right hand,*
> *That I may not be shaken*
> *Therefore my heart rejoiced, and*
> *My tongue was glad;*
> *Moreover my flesh also will rest in hope.'*
> Acts 2: 25

Here, we develop the heart of David in worship, while we are constantly being refreshed in the river of glory. This is a place of consecration, a place of sanctification that leads to exaltation and fascination with Jesus through illumination by and saturation in the Holy Spirit. This brings rejuvenation, celebration and jubilation in ever-increasing glory!

Our thankfulness has no bounds. We marvel at His goodness and grace that abounds over us constantly.

The magnitude of His Love overwhelms us, but at the same time, we enjoy this wondrous Love with fullness of joy. We now become channels of this divine love stream and we minister His love out of His Presence in the glory realm. Our capacity to love is enlarged as we pursue Him.

Now we come to experience that *"joy unspeakable and full of glory"* because of what He has done for us and attained for us on Calvary.

In the glory realm we are being changed into His image by His Holy Spirit and being filled to the fullness of God in Christ Jesus, being made one with the Trinity and being filled with His glory.

Let Him rejoice over you with singing, as you adore Him and worship Him in intimate abandonment to His love. Let every place in your heart be filled with worship. Live to glorify Him!

5. *His delight in us*

"Behold, you are fair, my love!
Behold you are fair!
You have dove's eyes behind your veil."

"You are all fair, my love,

And there is no spot in you."
"How fair is your love, My sister, my spouse!
How much better than wine is your love,
And the scent of your perfumes
Than all spices!

"Your lips, O my spouse,
Drip as the honeycomb;
Honey and milk are under your tongue;
And the fragrance of your garments
Is like the fragrance of Lebanon."
Song of Songs 4: 1,7, 10 -11

Our Beloved delights in our love adoration in intimate communion with Him.

The Lord rejoices over us with singing when we *will* to enjoy Him and rejoice in our knowledge of Him in who He is and what he has done for us on the cross. Our joy is also in His person, His power, His glory, His victory, His love, His Word and His wondrous working in our lives and many more.

When we sit or kneel in His presence without asking anything, but simply enjoying His Presence and pouring out our heart to Him in joyful adoration in exuberant praise, it will cause a celebration of angels in heaven.

He becomes our Song and our Joy!

We have entered into the Feast of Tabernacles, continually enjoying His Presence.

11

Plans and Strategies of the Enemy of Our Souls

Once we have entered the "Glory Realm," we should be sensitive to the nudging of the Holy Spirit, warning us of the plans and strategies of the devil. We must stay in touch with the Lord's emotions.

> *"Be sober, be vigilant; because your adversary the devil walks about like a roaring lion, seeking whom he may devour."*
> 1 Peter 5:8

Our greatest enemy though, is not the devil, but our carnal nature, the old man or the self. Both have one object – to destroy the life of Christ in us.

Haman represents both these aspects. If the devil can get hold of our flesh, he will have an open door to steal, kill and destroy.

Esther though, has been trained in sensitivity and obedience to Mordecai, who watches over her at the gates of the city all the time, representing the Holy Spirit – watching at the gates of our soul.

We have to be tuned in to the emotions of the Holy Spirit and, sensing that He is grieved, we have to enquire from Him to disclose to us the strategies and plans of the devil against God's elect and act upon it in intercession. He might choose you to be the vessel through which He will make intercession for others with groanings that cannot be uttered. (Romans 8: 26)

Haman portrays the pride of the flesh that wants to usurp authority and bring God's people in idolatrous worship of self. It is rebellion against the Holy Spirit and if we should submit to it, the devil will destroy us. We cannot bow before the Haman of our flesh.

When Esther is warned of the conspiracy of Haman, she is alarmed for herself and her people.

Mordecai assures her that if she would try to save her own life, she would lose it and God would raise up someone else to answer the call. Thus Esther also has to subdue **her** flesh and let the Spirit rule.

> *"Yet, who knows whether you have come to the kingdom for such a time as this?"*
> *Esther 4: 14*

Are you prepared to follow the guidance of the Holy Spirit — even if it could cost you your life?

Then Esther told them to reply to Mordecai:

> "Go, gather all the Jews who are present in Shushan, and fast for me; neither eat nor drink for three days, night or day. My maids and I will fast likewise. And so I will go to the king, which is against the law:
> ### and if I perish, I perish!"
>
> *Esther 4: 15-17*

The Holy Spirit will raise up a remnant to intercede with us and fast with us and for us to fulfill our call and His purpose for souls to be saved!

When she answers the call of the Holy Spirit to intervene on behalf of her people, she immediately enters into prayer, fasting and intercession, together with her maidservants and all of her people to seek the face of God.

> *"If My people who are called by My name*
> *will humble themselves,*
> *and pray and seek My face,*
> *and turn from their wicked ways, then I will*
> *hear from heaven, and will forgive*
> *their sin and heal their land."*
>
> *2 Chronicles 7:14*

This was an act of worship by humbling herself in obedience to the Holy Spirit in willingness to lay down her life (her flesh) for her people.

Fasting is one of the most powerful weapons of spiritual warfare against the enemy of our souls. It *opens* our ears to hear God's divine strategy for the situation and sensitizes us to the nudgings of the Holy Spirit.

The Lord often confronts us with the dark places of our lives in order to light our candles to bring the light to dark places and situations, without any desire for personal glory. Through compassion for her people the fire is kindled in her to rise to the call to fulfill her destiny!

Esther's three day fast also points to the death and resurrection of Jesus. She arises with the "Third Day" resurrection power of the Holy Spirit's anointing to lift death off her people!

12

ౚ౧ౚ౦

Prophetic Worship

In the glory of His Presence, we are tuned into the heart, mind and emotions of God through the Holy Spirit where we hear His heart beat, His desires and sense His emotions. Divine revelation and strategy is poured into our spirits and Word seeds are planted in us by the Holy Spirit that will produce a harvest as we prophesy that Word at the Mercy seat. The High Priest of our confession takes it to the Father and the Triune God broods over it and is watchful over His Word to perform it at the appointed time.

In this realm our vision is broadened and we do not ask only for ourselves, but we ask for the nations. The labor pains of intercession bring forth the harvest.

> *"Ask of Me, and I will give You the nations*
> *for Your inheritance."*
>
> Psalm 2:8

Prophetic visions are released in His Presence in the glory realm, which must be called into manifestation prophetically.

> *" calling those things that be not, just as though they were ."*
>
> Romans 4:17

Hear from the Godhead the Word for the situation and prophesy it over people, situations and nations. The High Priest of our Intercession, Jesus, intercedes with us at the Throne of Grace that at the appointed time we will receive help in need (Hebrews 4: 14).

Esther received divine insight, wisdom and strategy to expose the works of the enemy.

Fly on the wind of the Spirit; fly high in the power of His praises. Sing new intimate love songs born of the Spirit. Soar in the Spirit, like an eagle, into higher dimensions of His glory in ascension power and take dominion over the works of the enemy! What you can "see" from that vantage point, you can have! "See" the harvest fields and the souls that are ready to be harvested and prophesy salvation and deliverance and healing over the nations! Ask for laborers in the field and intercede for those who are laboring already. Whatever you ask the Father in the glory realm in His Name, He will give you if you believe!

> *We have to wake up to the call for the lost in our families, cities, countries and the world.*

Esther was pleading in intercession and fasting for the lives of her people and received divine strategy from God. This type of fasting is a statement of willingness to lay down your life for your brethren.

The time has come for the body of Christ to take hands in unity over barriers of denomination, race, color and country in unity of corporate intercession for the end-time harvest of souls and for revival to be poured out!

> *"Now it happened on the third day that Esther*
> *put on her royal robes and stood in the inner court*
> *of the king's palace, across from the king's house,*
> *while the king sat on his royal throne in the royal house,*
> *facing the entrance of the house."*
>
> Esther 5: 1

She had already put her life on the altar when she took up the call. Now, on the third day, she rises up in resurrection power of the Holy Spirit in the kingly authority with her royal robes, signifying the victory in full assurance of faith that she has the favor of the king and that the battle had already been won in the spiritual spheres on her knees. This is the faith of the Third Day overcoming Church that we can walk in!

> *"Yea, though I walk through the valley*
> *of the shadow of death*
> *I will fear no evil;*
> *For You are with me;*
> *Your rod and Your staff,*
> *they comfort me."*
>
> Psalm 23: 4

Esther's advantage was that she knew the king's heart towards her because she had previously found favor in his sight. Likewise we know the Bridegroom's heart towards us because we have already been in the Glory Realm in His Presence.

Esther knew that she was favored by the King of kings through a love relationship with Him and stood in faith that king Ahasuerus would extend his scepter of authority to her. In her weakness she depended upon the grace of God by faith.

When we come to the mercy seat with our desperate situations, we know the heart of the King and depend on His grace to give us favor.

We stand in reverence, clothed in our bridal robes we have received from Him, all glorious, but in the fear of our God.

> *"The royal daughter is all glorious within the palace;*
> *Her clothing is woven with gold"*
> *Psalm 45: 13*

We know that "gold" denotes character, which is the result of the preparation of the Bride through trials. The king knows that she has risked her life and she stands in humble submission, but in the integrity and truth of her conviction.

When we surrender our lives to the Lord, it is well pleasing to Him and He gives us His life in exchange. This signifies that the order and tradition of the law would be replaced by the new order of grace.

> *"You have ravished my heart,*
> *My sister, my spouse;*
> *You have ravished my heart*
> *With one look of your eyes*
> *With one link of your necklace."*
> *Song of Songs 4: 9*

The Lord reads the motives of our hearts through the windows of our souls as we are wearing His yoke with gentleness and lowliness of heart. The false burdens have been discarded and we are yoked together with Him for the saving of souls.

> *"So it was, when the king saw Queen Esther standing in the court, that she found favor in his sight, and the king held out to Esther the golden scepter that was in his hand. Then Esther went near and touched the top of the scepter."*
> *Esther 5: 2*

Her attitude of thankfulness and subjection is expressed in her touching the scepter, as well as her acceptance of his favor.

When we come into the King's Presence, it must be with an attitude of a humble heart, willing and waiting to hear His instructions and to be obedient to do what He requires of us. At the same time the pointing of the scepter signifies that the king is giving her acknowledgement as his bride and his favor abounds over her to give her the desires of her heart because of her attitude of submission to him.

And the king said to her,
"What do you wish, Queen Esther? What is your request? It shall be given to you – up to half the kingdom!"
Esther 5: 3

"If you abide in Me, and My words abide in you, you will ask what you desire, and it shall be done for you."
John 15: 7

"… heirs with God and joint heirs with Christ"
Romans 8: 17

We have an inheritance with Christ to rule and reign with Him over the works of the enemy. He has extended the rod of His authority to us that we can

"trample on snakes and scorpions, and over all the power of the enemy, and nothing shall by any means hurt us."
Luke 10: 19

Esther's first request is for the king and Haman to come to a banquet.

"So Esther answered, "If it pleases the king, let the king and Haman come today to the banquet that I have prepared."
Esther 5: 4

Often we just storm into the presence of God with no reverence, just to make our requests known to Him. Are we exercising "our rights" again, forgetting that we are in the Presence of the Almighty God who is worthy of all honor, glory and praise?

God wants us to honor Him in reverence and worship Him in the fear of the Lord, presenting a love feast to Him before we bring our requests and desires before Him.

13

Feasting with the King in the Presence of My Enemies

Let us wait on Him, as a waiter would, serving Him with our love offerings. Be sensitive to the Holy Spirit to lead you and guide you as Esther. Lay the table with your personal, heartfelt worship and adoration and invite Him to sup with you. Worship Him with your offerings of adoration prepared with fragrant spices in which He can delight.

Let Him feast on the love wine that comes from the crushed grapes of your wine press and ravish His heart with your dove-like eyes and the links of your necklace (Song of Solomon 4: 9).

"I have come to my garden,
My sister, my spouse;
I have gathered my myrrh with my spice
I have eaten my honeycomb
With my honey;
I have drunk my wine with my milk".

Song of Songs 5: 1

O, may what He finds in us be sweet tasting like honey!

In the Presence of the King all the hidden impurities and motives of our soulish realm come into the light.

> *"The heart is deceitful above all things,*
> *and desperately wicked; who can know it?*
> *I, the Lord, search the heart, I test the mind,*
> *Even to give every man according To his ways,*
> *According to the fruit of his doings."*
> *Jeremiah 17: 9-10*

Enjoying the glorious grace of the Lord can sometimes make us puffed up in pride and boasting thinking that we have "arrived." It can bring comparison with others who are "not like us", making us feel that we are better or more advanced. We might even disdainfully laugh at those who do not "understand" what we have. These feelings and thoughts creep in, in a very subtle way. All these attributes belong to Haman (representing the flesh) who is the enemy of the Spirit life.

We ask with David:

> *"Give me a clean heart o God,*
> *And renew a steadfast spirit within me."*
> *Psalm 51: 10*

We invite the King to a banquet of wine, poured out before Him over the offering of our lives with the purpose and intent to expose every work of the enemy of our souls.

In my fellowship with Him
> *"at the banqueting table, His banner over me is Love."*
> *Song of Songs 2:4*

At the first banquet Esther allows Haman to show forth

all his false pretenses, but when the king asks her what her request was, she answers:

> "If I have found favor in the sight of the king, and if it pleases the king to grant my petition, and to perform my request, let the king and Haman come to the banquet that I shall prepare for them, and I will do tomorrow as the king hath said."
>
> Esther 5: 8

Although a whole world is waiting to be saved, there comes a time when we realize that it is more important to minister to the Lord in the inner court than to minister to people in the outer court.

Our willingness to spend time with Him first and foremost, without asking anything for ourselves or our loved ones or our situations, to have communion with Him and invite Him to feast at the banqueting table of our love-worship-offerings, makes Him delight in us and

> "rejoice over us with gladness...
> and with singing."
>
> Zephaniah 3: 17

When we worship the Triune God, the favor of His grace abounds over us in the Glory Cloud.

> "...if anyone is a worshiper of God and does His will,
> He hears him."
>
> John 9: 31

His heart is touched beyond our imagination by a heart that really yearns for Him more than anything else in an abandonment of love.

As I look into His eyes with lovesick adoration, I see my own impurities in the beauty of His holiness and I eagerly repent in order to be washed and cleansed by His blood, while being enveloped in the Glory Cloud.

There is a twofold exposure of Haman in the Light of Truth – that of the subtlety of the carnal nature on the one hand, but also the plans, strategies and schemes of the evil one against God's people on the other.

I do not fear the shame of the carnal nature that will be exposed in His light, because His love has already made provision for me to be cleansed and washed that my bridal attire can be without spot or wrinkle. And I welcome the washing of my feet from the defilement of the world in which I walk daily, but which I am not a part of anymore.

In the Holy Place we have mainly dealt with externals and justified ourselves by weak excuses and comparisons with others, stating that we are not perfect.

In the Holy of Holies we come into the presence of the King with the pre-calculated agenda to expose the flesh in its finest subtleties and to bring it to death on the cross.

By the water washing of His Word and the reflection of His glory on my life as I worship Him, my presumptuous sins, unrighteous agendas, false motives, covetousness, pride and deceitfulness are brought into the light by His love.

As my *new man* unflinchingly agrees with the Holy Spirit to put to death the works of the flesh, I am being changed into His image to grow up

"to the measure of the stature of the fullness of Christ."
Ephesians 4:13

All our "issues" have to be taken to the cross, tied up and brought to death. True sanctification is when the issues of my life are crucified, justified by the spilling of blood and then glorified by the Spirit.

The issue of His righteousness must touch everything on this plane in order for it to be justified and glorified.

Something cannot be eternal if it is not righteous.

I am sewing a garment of praise for Eternity.

All the shields and walls I have built around myself for "self" protection must be torn down. They are mainly called pride, being unteachable and self-righteousness. The carnal armor of self-power and own ability is shed as we put on God's armor of the Spirit (Ephesians 6).

Trusting in self brings us under a curse, but trusting in God brings the blessings. (Jeremiah 17: 5-8)

> *"And on the second day, at the banquet of wine, the king again said to Esther, "What is your petition, Queen Esther? It shall be granted you. And what is your request, up to half the kingdom? It shall be done!"*
>
> Esther 7: 2

The heart of the king trusts her so much that he will grant her anything. She has now found favor in the presence of her enemy.

> *"Delight yourself also in the Lord, And He shall give you the desires of your heart."*
>
> Psalm 37: 4

"Then Queen Esther answered and said, "If I have found favor

in your sight, O king, and if it pleases the king,
let my life be given me at my petition,
and my people at my request"
Esther 7: 3

"for the law of the Spirit of life in Christ Jesus
has made me free from the law of sin and death"
Romans 8:2

Like Esther, I lay down my flesh to receive His life and I willingly expose Haman's nature. In His Presence there is no tolerance of sin - the verdict is death on the gallows. Mordecai, who would not bow before Haman, is now given the royal robe, the royal crown and the king's horse. This indicates that the puffed up, prideful flesh has bowed down before the rule of the Holy Spirit.

At the same time the enemy's schemes of wickedness against my loved ones and God's people are brought into the light.

We now see maturity in Esther – she is no longer intimidated by the thought of death, but there is an adamant resolve in her petition – Haman will no more be tolerated! The king's wrath brings the verdict: Haman will hang on his own gallows!

"I will deliver you from the hand of the wicked
And I will redeem you from the grip of the terrible."
Jeremiah 15:21

14

Victory Over the Enemy

Through our victory over the flesh and our submission to the Holy Spirit, we receive a greater measure of anointing and authority over the works of the devil.

> *"On that day king Ahasuerus gave Queen Esther the house of Haman, the enemy of the Jews. And Mordecai came before the king, for Esther had told how he was related to her. So the king took off his signet ring, which he had taken from Haman, and gave it to Mordecai; and Esther appointed Mordecai over the house of Haman."*
>
> Esther 8: 1-2

It is significant that Esther appointed Mordecai over the house of Haman and the decree was written according to what Mordecai commanded. Esther has surrendered all to the control and dictates of the Holy Spirit.

In His Presence we are empowered by waiting on Him to rise up like eagles on the wings of the Spirit to fly high in the warmth of the Son – easily able to discern the snakes from our great height, pick them up and smash them to pieces on the Rock.

"Now Esther spoke again to the king, fell down at his feet, and implored him with tears to counteract the evil of Haman the Agagite, and the scheme which he had devised against the Jews."
Esther 8: 3

When we spend much time in the Presence of the King, our faith grows in boldness against the enemy and we are moved with compassion for the people to intercede with travailing in tears, bowing in dependence and trust before the One who holds all the power and authority in His hands.

"And the king held out the golden scepter toward Esther…"
Esther 8:4

When we worship the Triune God, the favor of His grace abounds over us in the Glory Cloud. Worship brings you to the mercy seat of God – it is the meeting place between God and man through the Blood. **He will meet with us in mercy when we worship Him.**

In the New Covenant through the shed Blood of Jesus, He becomes our "mercy seat" at the Throne of Grace. It is the throne of both God and the Lamb and God's redemptive plan fulfils the law. The blood of Jesus was brought before God's throne as a propitiation for our sins.

The place of mercy is the costliest place in the universe **– it cost Him everything!**

The Son is the outpouring of God's glory, the Son is the speaking and giving of His Mercy!

Therefore, when I abide in Him as He in me, I can ask **anything** in the **NAME OF JESUS – AND IT SHALL BE GIVEN TO ME (John 15).**

He redeemed us from the curse through His Holy blood – by **HIS MERCY – which endures forever!**

The Mercy Seat is the place of intercession of the Son for us.

"He always lives to make intercession for us"

Hebrews 7: 25

The Mercy Seat is the place of **HIS PRESENCE!**

The Mercy Seat is where His Holy Spirit is poured out even as His Shikinah Glory hovered over the cherubim on the mercy seat above the Ark of the Covenant.

Strength and Glory is obtained in His Presence.

When I come to the Mercy Seat and accept the payment for every bill in my life through the Blood of the Lamb, the Holy Spirit empowers my redemption through the Name of Jesus.

I can put every situation on the mercy seat and call on His mercy to come to my rescue through the intercession of my High Priest, Jesus.

The glory and the goodness of God flow in the river of His mercy.

Because of the Blood, "I can come forward with boldness to the Throne of Grace that I can receive mercy and find grace for timely help" (Hebrews 4: 16).

God's mercy reaches farther and bridges the gap between God's grace and His judgment and is always available to us.

However, we need to receive and find His mercy and grace by exercising our spirit in Praise to contact our High Priest, who is moved with compassion for all our weaknesses.

"Seeing then that we have a great High Priest who has passed through the heavens, Jesus the Son of God, let us hold fast our confession For we do not have a High Priest who cannot sympathize with our weaknesses, but was in all points tempted as we are, yet without sin. Let us therefore come boldly to the throne of grace That we may obtain mercy and find grace to help in time of need."
Hebrews 4: 14-16

The Lord Jesus entered the heavens, the Holy of Holies within the veil, and in Him is the heavenly haven for our refuge, which we can now enter into by the Spirit.

Jesus, as our High Priest, stands before the Throne of Grace offering up His Holy Blood as the "reason" for mercy before the Father when we call on His mercy and Praise Him for His mercy that endureth forever. He is the High Priest after the order of Melchizedek, forever and ever (Hebrews 7).

The moment we start praising Him for His mercy, the enemy is led into ambush and destroys himself. (2 Chronicles 20).

Let our praises for the victory of the Blood of Jesus resound in heaven so that He can meet us in His mercy and we can find grace at the right moment for our desperate situations (Hebrews 4: 14).

Praise and worship brings punishment on God's enemies!

"Let the high praises of God be in their mouth,
And a two-edged sword in their hand,
To execute vengeance on the nations;
And punishment on the peoples;
To bind their kings with chains,
And their nobles with fetters of iron;

> *To execute on them the written judgment –*
> *This honor have all the saints.*
> *Praise the Lord!"*
>
> Psalm 149:6-9

We come in agreement with the Word through faith and proclaim, pray, praise, prophesy or call that Word into manifestation at the mercy seat because of the Blood. In any situation of our life, the High Priest of our confession brings that Word before the Throne of Grace and

> *"He is watchful over His Word to perform it!"*
> (Jeremiah 1: 12)

even by the angels that are sent forth (Psalm 103: 12) and that
> *"Word will not return to Him void"*
> (Isaiah 55: 11)

When we abide in the Word, and abide in His love, we can ask the Father anything in the Name of Jesus, and we will receive it in due time.

> *" but if anyone is a worshiper of God and does His will,*
> *He hears him."*
> John 9: 31

Esther has holy boldness against the enemy, as the king's favor is extended to her, to rise up and stand before the him, but her attitude is that of total humility and dependence, without any presumption (Esther 8:5). Her motivation is a heart of love, mercy and compassion for her people.

> *"For how can I endure to see the evil that will come to*
> *my people? Or how can I endure to see the destruction*
> *of my countrymen?"*
> Esther 8:6

This reveals the heart of an intercessor and moves the heart of God. In the resurrection power of the Holy Spirit we are given the power to crush satan under our feet and destroy his evil works in the Name of the King.

"And he (Mordecai) wrote in the name of the King Ahasueros,
sealed it with the king's signet ring, and sent letters
by couriers on horseback, riding on royal horses
bred from swift steeds. By these letters the king permitted the
Jews who were in every city to gather together and protect
their lives – ***To destroy, kill, and annihilate*** *All the forces*
of any people or province that would assault them, both little
children and women, and to plunder their possessions."
- Esther 8: 10-11

Esther asked for life – for her people and herself. As a result of God's mercy the decrees were served to the people – ("it is written") and sealed with the king's seal! The Bride with the authority of the King's seal becomes a worshipping warrior!

"The Jews had light and gladness, joy and honor.
And in every province and city, wherever the king's command
and decree came, the Jews had joy and gladness, a feast and a
holiday. Then many of the people of the land became Jews,
because fear of the Jews fell upon them."
- Esther 8: 16-17

The Blood of the Lamb has delivered us from every decree or curse of destruction written against us by the enemy.

As we are sent out with His Word, according to the great commission (Mark 16: 15-18), sealed by the authority of His Name and His Blood, we will be part of the royal army that brings the Good News of the Gospel of Salvation in Christ Jesus to the world.

> *"Thus the Jews defeated all their enemies*
> *with the stroke of the sword, with slaughter*
> *and destruction, and did what they pleased*
> *with those who hated them."*
> *- Esther 9: 5*

Many people are suffering oppression because they do not know the power of the sword of the Spirit, the Word of God (Ephesians 6: 17) or the authority that has been given to us in Jesus' Name and by His blood.

When we abide in His Presence, abide in the Word, and abide in His love, we can ask the Father anything in the Name of Jesus, and we WILL RECEIVE IT IN **DUE TIME**.

Let us polish our Sword and become saturated with the Word of God to use it effectively against the enemy of our souls.

After the victory the Jews
> *"celebrated the fourteenth day of the month of Adar*
> *with gladness and feasting as a holiday,*
> *and for sending presents to one another."*
> *- Esther 9: 19*

This feast is still celebrated today among the Jews in memory of the victory against the schemes of Haman.

When the Holy Spirit is given His rightful place in our lives and in the Church, it is a time of gladness and feasting. We will always have the victory over the flesh and over our enemies through the power of the Holy Spirit. And we will become givers through the manifold graces of the Lord. We will rejoice and feast at the table of the Lord in the presence of our enemies and our cup will run over (Psalm 23: 5).

"God's got an army marching through this land,

> *Deliverance is their song*
> *There's healing in their hands*
> *Everlasting joy and gladness in their hearts*
> *And in this army I've got a part."*

We can constantly rejoice in the victory of Jesus on Calvary!

This joy and gladness in Him is an aroma of death to the enemy of our souls.

Let our lives become a walk of worship and a house of prayer and intercession while feasting with Him at the table continuously and then going out on His word in the power of the Holy Spirit to confound the plans of the enemy and win souls for the Kingdom of God.

And lastly – let us keep His mercy and great works of deliverance in remembrance and tell our children and children's children of the wondrous works of our God so that His name can be glorified!

15

The Bride Without Spot or Wrinkle

As we yield to the Spirit, looking into the glory of the Lord, we are being transformed from *"glory to glory"* into **His image - spirit, soul and body – unto maturity** - growing up into the full stature of Christ. This is the path of sanctification. The old creation and the natural life have been sanctified by the Holy Spirit with God's life and God's holy nature for the glory of His praise.

Thus God is preparing for His Son a Bride – spotless and without wrinkle – in this life to be seated with Him in heavenly places in authority over the works of the devil and in eternity to be joined to Him at the marriage supper of the Lamb. Thereafter we will rule and reign with Him victoriously.

> *"...Christ also loved the church and gave Himself*
> *for her, that He might sanctify and cleanse her with*
> *the washing of water by the word, that He might*
> *present her to Himself a glorious church,*
> *not having spot or wrinkle or any such thing but that*
> *she should be holy and without blemish."*
> *Ephesians 5: 25-27*

The company of the Bride is described as *"those who overcome"* in the Book of Revelation and these are the promises to "overcomers:"

Rev. 2: 7	*"to eat of the tree of life"*
Rev. 2: 11	*"given a crown of life"* and *"not be hurt of the second death"*
Rev. 2: 17	*"to eat of the hidden manna"* and *"to be given a white stone and* *"a new name"*
Rev. 2: 26	*"power over the nations to rule"* *"given the morning star"*
Rev. 3: 5	*"clothed in white"* and *"name not blotted our of the Book of Life"*
Rev. 3: 12	*"a pillar in the temple of God"* and *"I will write on them My new name"*
Rev. 3: 21	*"sit with God and the Lamb in the throne"*
Rev. 21: 7	*"inherit all things"*

"And the Spirit and the Bride say,
Come! And let him who hears say,
Come!
And let him who thirsts come.
Whoever desires let him take of
the water of life freely."
— Revelation 22: 17